Marco Polo
and the Medieval Explorers

General Editor

William H. Goetzmann
Jack S. Blanton, Sr., Chair in History
  University of Texas at Austin

Consulting Editor

Tom D. Crouch
Chairman, Department of Aeronautics
  National Air and Space Museum
  Smithsonian Institution

WORLD EXPLORERS

Marco Polo
and the Medieval Explorers

Rebecca Stefoff

Introductory Essay by Michael Collins

CHELSEA HOUSE PUBLISHERS

New York · Philadelphia

On the cover   Detail of a map of Asia from the 1375 *Catalan Atlas*; Varese's portrait of Marco Polo

Chelsea House Publishers
Editor-in-Chief   Remmel Nunn
Managing Editor   Karyn Gullen Browne
Copy Chief   Mark Rifkin
Picture Editor   Adrian G. Allen
Art Director   Maria Epes
Assistant Art Director   Noreen Romano
Series Design   Loraine Machlin
Manufacturing Director   Gerald Levine
Systems Manager   Lindsey Ottman
Production Manager   Joseph Romano
Production Coordinator   Marie Claire Cebrián

World Explorers
Senior Editor   Sean Dolan

Staff for MARCO POLO AND THE MEDIEVAL EXPLORERS
Copy Editor   Christopher Duffy
Editorial Assistant   Martin Mooney
Picture Researcher   Alan Gottlieb
Senior Designer   Basia Niemczyc

First Printing

1   3   5   7   9   8   6   4   2

Library of Congress Cataloging-in-Publication Data

Stefoff, Rebecca
    Marco Polo and the medieval explorers/Rebecca Stefoff.
        p.   cm.—(World explorers)
    Includes bibliographical references (p.   ) and index.
    Summary: Examines the life and travels of the medieval explorer.
    ISBN 0-7910-1294-8
        0-7910-1519-X (pbk.)
    1. Polo, Marco, ca. 1254–1324—Journeys—Juvenile literature.
2. Voyages and travels—Juvenile literature.   3. Explorers—Italy—
Biography—Juvenile literature.   4. China—Description and
travel—to 1900—Juvenile.   [1. Polo, Marco, ca. 1254–1324
2. Explorers.   3. Voyages and travels.]   I. Title.   II. Series.
                                                        91-14049
G370.P9S74   1992   CIP
910'.92—dc20   AC

CONTENTS

WORLD EXPLORERS

THE EARLY EXPLORERS

Herodotus and the Explorers of the Classical Age
Marco Polo and the Medieval Explorers
The Viking Explorers

THE FIRST GREAT AGE OF DISCOVERY

Jacques Cartier, Samuel de Champlain, and the Explorers of Canada
Christopher Columbus and the First Voyages to the New World
From Coronado to Escalante: The Explorers of the Spanish Southwest
Hernando de Soto and the Explorers of the American South
Sir Francis Drake and the Struggle for an Ocean Empire
Vasco da Gama and the Portuguese Explorers
La Salle and the Explorers of the Mississippi
Ferdinand Magellan and the Discovery of the World Ocean
Pizarro, Orellana, and the Exploration of the Amazon
The Search for the Northwest Passage
Giovanni da Verrazano and the Explorers of the Atlantic Coast

THE SECOND GREAT AGE OF DISCOVERY

Roald Amundsen and the Quest for the South Pole
Daniel Boone and the Opening of the Ohio Country
Captain James Cook and the Explorers of the Pacific
The Explorers of Alaska
John Charles Frémont and the Great Western Reconnaissance
Alexander von Humboldt, Colossus of Exploration
Lewis and Clark and the Route to the Pacific
Alexander Mackenzie and the Explorers of Canada
Robert Peary and the Quest for the North Pole
Zebulon Pike and the Explorers of the American Southwest
John Wesley Powell and the Great Surveys of the American West
Jedediah Smith and the Mountain Men of the American West
Henry Stanley and the European Explorers of Africa
Lt. Charles Wilkes and the Great U.S. Exploring Expedition

THE THIRD GREAT AGE OF DISCOVERY

Apollo to the Moon
The Explorers of the Undersea World
The First Men in Space
The Mission to Mars and Beyond
Probing Deep Space

CHELSEA HOUSE PUBLISHERS

Into the Unknown

Michael Collins

It is difficult to define most eras in history with any precision, but not so the space age. On October 4, 1957, it burst on us with little warning when the Soviet Union launched *Sputnik*, a 184-pound cannonball that circled the globe once every 96 minutes. Less than 4 years later, the Soviets followed this first primitive satellite with the flight of Yuri Gagarin, a 27-year-old fighter pilot who became the first human to orbit the earth. The Soviet Union's success prompted President John F. Kennedy to decide that the United States should "land a man on the moon and return him safely to earth" before the end of the 1960s. We now had not only a space age but a space race.

I was born in 1930, exactly the right time to allow me to participate in Project Apollo, as the U.S. lunar program came to be known. As a young man growing up, I often found myself too young to do the things I wanted—or suddenly too old, as if someone had turned a switch at midnight. But for Apollo, 1930 was the perfect year to be born, and I was very lucky. In 1966 I enjoyed circling the earth for three days, and in 1969 I flew to the moon and laughed at the sight of the tiny earth, which I could cover with my thumbnail.

How the early explorers would have loved the view from space! With one glance Christopher Columbus could have plotted his course and reassured his crew that the world was indeed round. In 90 minutes Magellan could have looked down at every port of call in the *Victoria*'s three-year circumnavigation of the globe. Given a chance to map their route from orbit, Lewis and Clark could have told President Jefferson that there was no easy Northwest Passage but that a continent of exquisite diversity awaited their scrutiny.

In a physical sense, we have already gone to most places that we can. That is not to say that there are not new adventures awaiting us deep in the sea or on the red plains of Mars, but more important than reaching new places will be understanding those we have already visited. There are vital gaps in our understanding of how our planet works as an ecosystem and how our planet fits into the infinite order of the universe. The next great age may well be the age of assimilation, in which we use microscope and tele-scope to evaluate what we have discovered and put that knowledge to use. The adventure of being first to reach may be replaced by the satisfaction of being first to grasp. Surely that is a form of exploration as vital to our well-being, and perhaps even survival, as the distinction of being the first to explore a specific geographical area.

The explorers whose stories are told in the books of this series did not just sail perilous seas, scale rugged moun-tains, traverse blistering deserts, dive to the depths of the ocean, or land on the moon. Their voyages and expedi-tions were journeys of mind as much as of time and dis-tance, through which they—and all of mankind—were able to reach a greater understanding of our universe. That challenge remains, for all of us. The imperative is to see, to understand, to develop knowledge that others can use, to help nurture this planet that sustains us all. Perhaps being born in 1975 will be as lucky for a new generation of explorer as being born in 1930 was for Neil Armstrong, Buzz Aldrin, and Mike Collins.

The Reader's Journey

William H. Goetzmann

This volume is one of a series that takes us with the great explorers of the ages on bold journeys over the oceans and the continents and into outer space. As we travel along with these imaginative and courageous journeyers, we share their adventures and their knowledge. We also get a glimpse of that mysterious and inextinguishable fire that burned in the breast of men such as Magellan and Columbus—the fire that has propelled all those throughout the ages who have been driven to leave behind family and friends for a voyage into the unknown.

No one has ever satisfactorily explained the urge to explore, the drive to go to the "back of beyond." It is certain that it has been present in man almost since he began walking erect and first ventured across the African savannas. Sparks from that same fire fueled the transoceanic explorers of the Ice Age, who led their people across the vast plain that formed a land bridge between Asia and North America, and the astronauts and scientists who determined that man must reach the moon.

Besides an element of adventure, all exploration involves an element of mystery. We must not confuse exploration with discovery. Exploration is a purposeful human activity—a search for something. Discovery may be the end result of that search; it may also be an accident, as when Columbus found a whole new world while searching for the Indies. Often, the explorer may not even realize the full significance of what he has discovered, as was the case with Columbus. Exploration, on the other hand, is the product of a cultural or individual curiosity; it is a unique process that has enabled mankind to know and understand the world's oceans, continents, and polar regions. It is at the heart of scientific thinking. One of its most significant aspects is that it teaches people to ask the right questions; by doing so, it forces us to reevaluate what we think we know and understand. Thus knowledge progresses, and we are driven constantly to a new awareness and appreciation of the universe in all its infinite variety.

The motivation for exploration is not always pure. In his fascination with the new, man often forgets that others have been there before him. For example, the popular notion of the discovery of America overlooks the complex Indian civilizations that had existed there for thousands of years before the arrival of Europeans. Man's desire for conquest, riches, and fame is often linked inextricably with his quest for the unknown, but a story that touches so closely on the human essence must of necessity treat war as well as peace, avarice with generosity, both pride and humility, frailty and greatness. The story of exploration is above all a story of humanity and of man's understanding of his place in the universe.

The WORLD EXPLORERS series has been divided into four sections. The first treats the explorers of the ancient world, the Viking explorers of the 9th through the 11th centuries, and Marco Polo and the medieval explorers. The rest of the series is divided into three great ages of exploration. The first is the era of Columbus and Magellan: the period spanning the 15th and 16th centuries, which saw the discovery and exploration of the New World and the world ocean. The second might be called the age of science and imperialism, the era made possible by the scientific advances of the 17th century, which witnessed the discovery of the world's last two undiscovered continents, Australia and Antarctica, the mapping of all the continents and oceans, and the establishment of colonies all over the world. The third great age refers to the most ambitious quests of the 20th century—the probing of space and of the ocean's depths.

As we reach out into the darkness of outer space and other galaxies, we come to better understand how our ancestors confronted *oecumene*, or the vast earthly unknown. We learn once again the meaning of an unknown 18th-century sea captain's advice to navigators:

> And if by chance you make a landfall on the shores of another sea in a far country inhabited by savages and barbarians, remember you this: the greatest danger and the surest hope lies not with fires and arrows but in the quicksilver hearts of men.

At its core, exploration is a series of moral dramas. But it is these dramas, involving new lands, new people, and exotic ecosystems of staggering beauty, that make the explorers' stories not only moral tales but also some of the greatest adventure stories ever recorded. They represent the process of learning in its most expansive and vivid forms. We see that real life, past and present, transcends even the adventures of the starship *Enterprise*.

In the Court
of the Great Khan

Sometime in early 1275, three travelers approached the city of Shang-du, in northeastern China. The wayfarers were two brothers named Nicolo and Maffeo Polo and Nicolo's son Marco, a young man of about 20. History does not record what they said or felt as they drew near their destination, but it is likely that they were weary from their journey and eager to reach Shang-du, for they had been traveling for three and a half years since leaving their home, halfway around the world, in Venice, Italy. They had witnessed countless marvels on the road, but none of the sights they had seen was more splendid than Shang-du itself.

The city had been built in three sections. Its outermost district consisted of a hollow square surrounded by walls of packed earth 12 to 18 feet high; these walls were pierced by 6 gates and surmounted by 6 tall watchtowers. Each side of this square was nearly a mile long. Within the walls of the outer city, more than 100,000 people lived in houses made of boards or mud bricks.

Within the square formed by the outer city was another wall, this one made of brick, more than 10 feet high and about 2,000 feet long on each of its 4 sides. Inside this wall stood the inner city of Shang-du, a cluster of palaces and imposing government buildings surrounded by gardens and fountains. In the center of the inner city rose a high platform of rock and earth upon which stood the

Nicolo and Maffeo Polo depart Constantinople in 1260 on their first trip to the Far East. Eleven years later the Polo brothers would return to Cathay with Niccolo's son Marco. This illustration is from a 15th-century French version of Marco Polo's account of his adventures.

A Yuan, or Mongol, dynasty painting of a T'ang-era palace. The Mongol rulers of China were regarded by the native Chinese as usurpers and outsiders, but Marco found Khubilai Khan, the Mongol emperor, to be an almost model ruler. Marco said that the khan's palace in the city of Khan-balik "was the greatest palace that ever was."

Pavilion of Great Harmony—the imperial palace of Khubilai Khan, the Great Khan of the Mongols and the ruler of China and most of Asia. Made of marble and other ornamental stones, "its halls and rooms and passages," Marco was to remember years later, were "all gilded and wonderfully painted within with pictures and images of beasts and birds and trees and flowers and many kinds of things, so well and so cunningly that it is a delight to see."

The third district of Shang-du had been designed by Khubilai Khan to recall the homeland of his nomadic ancestors on the grassy, open steppes, or plains, of Mongolia. It was a vast enclosed park, complete with hills, meadows, and streams and stocked with deer and other game animals—the private hunting ground of Khubilai and his guests, who chased their quarry on horseback with falcons and tame hunting leopards, or cheetahs. Herds of snow-white horses, the cherished property of the Great Khan, roamed the hunting park. At its center was a palace cleverly constructed of cane and painted with gold; the palace roof was upheld by pillars in the shape of enormous rearing dragons. This cane palace was anchored to the ground by 200 silk cables and, as Marco was to discover, could be moved from place to place within the park at the whim of the khan.

This was Shang-du, the splendid summer residence of Khubilai Khan, who spent the months of June, July, and August there to escape the stifling heat of Khan-balik, his other capital city. When Marco Polo first saw it, Shang-du was a young city, created by the Great Khan only 15 years before, but the vivid impression it made on the young Venetian traveler would help make it immortal. Marco called the exotic city "Ciandu"; more than five centuries later, in 1798, the English poet Samuel Taylor Coleridge would use this name, altered slightly to Xanadu, in his classic poem "Kubla Khan," which begins

In Xanadu did Kubla Khan
A stately pleasure dome decree:
Where Alph, the sacred river, ran

Through caverns measureless to man
   Down to a sunless sea.
So twice five miles of fertile ground
With walls and towers were girdled round:
And there were gardens bright with sinuous rills,
Where blossomed many an incense-bearing tree;
And here were forests ancient as the hills,
Enfolding sunny spots of greenery.

To Coleridge in his humble cottage at Nether Stowey, far-off Xanadu was the very incarnation of imagination and mystery, but to the Polos in 1275, Shang-du was no poetic fancy but the end of a toilsome journey—and the fulfillment of a vow. Nicolo and Maffeo Polo had crossed the Asian continent from Italy once before to visit Khubilai Khan, and when they had left his court they had promised to return. Now they had done so, bringing with them not only Marco but a gift that had been especially requested by Khubilai: a container of oil from the lamp that was kept burning in the Church of the Holy Sepulchre in Jerusalem, where Christ was believed to have been buried.

With one of his hunting leopards (cheetahs) mounted behind him, Khubilai Khan unleashes a falcon after a stag, a wolf, and a wild boar. The khan kept virtually every conceivable variety of wild animal within the 16-mile wall of his private hunting compound, and 200 specially trained falcons resided in the greatest comfort in the imperial mews, where they supped regularly on venison.

The Great Khan was delighted to see the Polo brothers again. Indeed, he was so eager for their arrival that when he heard that they were approaching his court he sent servants and knights out to meet them some 40 days' travel on horseback from Shang-du. This escort not only protected the travelers from bandits but also provided them with everything they needed during the final stages of their journey. "By these means, and through the blessing of God," Marco said, "they were conveyed in safety to the royal court."

According to Marco, Khubilai greeted the Polos "graciously and honorably" at an assembly of his principal nobles. Having experience of Mongol court etiquette, the Polo brothers demonstrated their respect for the khan by performing the oriental bow sometimes called the kowtow: They knelt at full length and touched their foreheads to the floor. Khubilai at once told them to rise, and he then asked them to tell him of their adventures since he had last seen them, some seven or eight years before.

It has been to posterity's benefit that Marco was an exceptionally curious and observant young man, interested in the details of every new thing that he saw. On this day in Shang-du, he became one of only a handful of Europeans who had actually seen the Great Khan of the Mongols, a figure of virtually legendary stature back home in Italy. Years later, Marco recorded his impression of the Mongol leader with these words: "Let me tell you next of the personal appearance of the Great Lord of Lords whose name is Kubilai Khan. He is a man of good stature, neither short nor tall but of moderate height. His limbs are well fleshed out and modeled in due proportion. His complexion is fair and ruddy like a rose, the eyes black and handsome, the nose shapely and set squarely in place." Khubilai received the holy oil from Jerusalem "with joy," Marco said, "and gave directions that it should be preserved with religious care." It was only then that he took notice of Marco and asked who the young man was.

Khubilai Khan, by an unknown Ming dynasty artist. (The Ming dynasty refers to the period of native Chinese rule that followed the Mongol dynasty and lasted from 1368 to 1644.) The splendors of Khubilai's empire, as related by Marco Polo, inspired several generations of European explorers to attempt to reach the Far East.

"Sire," replied Nicolo Polo, "he is my son, and your liege man."

"He is heartily welcome," said Khubilai Khan.

With these simple and gracious words began a long and affectionate relationship between Khubilai Khan and Marco Polo. Khubilai was 60 years old when they met, Marco some 40 years younger. The Mongol warlord and the Italian merchant's son had very little in common— they shared neither religion, education, nor experience— yet each recognized and respected qualities possessed by the other. Marco Polo regarded Khubilai as a brave, wise, and just ruler—"the Great Khan is the wisest man and the ablest in all respects, the best ruler of subjects and of empire and the man of the highest character of all that have ever been," Polo said of him—and the khan soon noticed that Marco was both curious and clever, for the young man had learned at least two languages, Persian and Mongol, during his journey to Shang-du and was able to describe things he had seen in vivid detail. Khubilai enrolled Marco Polo among his knights and assigned him to a series of increasingly important missions that carried him to many corners of the far-flung Mongol Empire.

Marco Polo would remain a loyal and diligent member of Khubilai's court for about 17 years, until 1291 or 1292, when he and his father and uncle left China to return to Italy. The tales Marco told upon his return astonished his fellow Europeans, many of whom flatly refused to believe them. Eventually, Marco's account of his journeys, as told to a popular author of Arthurian romances, one Rusti-chello of Pisa, was published in a book that became one of history's first best-sellers and made him the world's most celebrated traveler. Seven centuries later, scholars still argue over how much of Marco Polo's book is fact and how much is fable, yet all agree that the Venetian voyager played the starring role in the centuries-long European and Asian drama of mutual discovery that unfolded in medieval times.

القرآن ثم أربع أساطير لها أو زخارف جلاها وقال اركبوا فيها بسم الله مجراها

ومرساها ثمة نفس نفس المغرمين أو عباد الله للكرمين وقال لك انا

The Unknown East

The China to which Marco Polo traveled was a world utterly unfamiliar to the Europeans of his time, nearly as alien and surprising as the Americas would seem upon their discovery by European mariners two centuries later. But Europe and Asia were not complete strangers to one another. Contact between the two ends of the Eurasian landmass had been taking place in one way or another since ancient times.

Trade thrived in the lands around the eastern end of the Mediterranean Sea and the Red Sea, a region sometimes referred to collectively as the Levant, as early as 1000 B.C. By that time, cities and ports in Asia Minor (present-day Turkey), Syria, Lebanon, Palestine, Egypt, Mesopotamia (now called Iraq), and Persia (modern-day Iran) and on the coast of Arabia were already centers of seaborne and overland merchant traffic from the Far East and Europe. With this merchandise traveled rumors, legends, and scraps of history and geography, often jumbled together and confused but generally accepted as fact. By the 4th century B.C., for example, the people of the Mediterranean had learned from the tales of Persian merchants and Arab sailors that somewhere on the far side of Persia lay India, a land of men with the heads of dogs, of diamond mountains where birds five times the size of men nested, of huge lizards that could drag whole oxen into rivers, and of kings who marched to war on elephants. The crocodiles

An Arab dhow, *a lateen-rigged (triangular sailed) sailing vessel. The Arabs were often the middlemen in the East-West trade.*

This ancient Roman fresco depicts grain being loaded onto a Mediterranean sailing ship. The ancient Romans called the Mediterranean the *mare* nostrum *or* mare internum, *meaning, basically, "our sea" or "the sea that is known to us." It was not until the Dark Ages—when under the influence of Christian dogma European geographic knowledge greatly diminished— that the waterway became known as the Mediterranean, which means literally "sea in the middle of the earth."*

and elephants were real, as travelers to India would eventually discover, but the giant birds and dog-headed men were not. This mixture of fact and fantasy was typical of geographic knowledge in Marco Polo's time and for a long time afterward.

One of the first Westerners to venture far into the mysterious East is generally remembered as a conqueror rather than as an explorer. He was Alexander the Great, ruler of Macedonia and Greece. In 334 B.C., at the age of 22, he set sail with his army for the Hellespont, traditionally regarded as the meeting point of East and West. Then, after supposedly paying homage at the grave of Achilles, the legendary hero of the Trojan War, Alexander led his force of 35,000 men east into Asia Minor to make war upon the powerful Persian Empire of Darius III, whose realm included several Greek-speaking colonies. After defeating Darius's vaunted forces in several battles in Turkey and Lebanon, Alexander moved south into Egypt, where in 332 he was deified and founded the city of Alexandria at the mouth of the Nile River. Now in possession of the western half of the Persian Empire, Alexander then led his army north and east through Mesopotamia and into Persia itself in pursuit of the fleeing Darius. At this point,

Alexander had crossed the boundary of the known world (known, that is, to Europeans) and entered uncharted territory. After routing Darius's much larger forces at the Battle of Gaugamela in Mesopotamia, Alexander took possession of the famed cities of Babylon, "the soul of the East"; Susa, Darius's administrative and financial center; and Persepolis, the capital of the realm, where he sacked the city and torched the magnificent palace of Xerxes.

Soon afterward, Alexander learned that Darius had been murdered by Bessus, the governor of the Persian province of Bactria, a region just north of the present-day border between the Soviet Union and Afghanistan and southwest of the Aral Sea. The rebellious Bessus was now trying to raise an army that would drive out the Greeks. Determined to crush this uprising before it could spread to other parts of his newly conquered empire, Alexander, who had taken for himself the grand titles Great King and Lord of Asia, led his own army north to Bactria. En route, the Greeks crossed one of the world's most rugged mountain ranges, the desolate Hindu Kush, through the Khawak Pass, which is more than 11,500 feet above sea level. After descending into Bactria, they easily disposed of Bessus and his forces, then spent the remainder of 328 cementing their control over Bactria. That task completed, Alexander turned his thoughts to new conquests, specifically a march into India. He took his army back over the Hindu Kush by a southeasterly route through present-day Afghanistan, subjugating the fiercely independent mountain tribes as he went. When the Greeks finally reached the headwaters of the Indus River, the boundary of India, Alexander's weary army—its numbers now greatly reduced by battle, exhaustion, and disease—refused to go on. Alexander was forced to turn back. Legend has it that the great warrior sat on the banks of the river and wept because there were no more worlds for him to conquer, but the indefatigable Alexander turned even his return to Persia into a journey of exploration.

In his 33 years, the Macedonian Alexander the Great—depicted here astride his horse Bucephalus in a mosaic found among the ruins of the demolished Italian city of Pompeii—conquered much of what was then the known world. When the complaints of his army finally forced him to halt at the Indus River, Alexander believed he was just a short march from the easternmost extent of the Asian continent.

First, he had the Greeks build a large fleet of boats, in which they set sail down the uncharted Indus. Upon reaching the river's mouth six months later, Alexander found himself on the shores of a sea unknown to the Greeks—the Indian Ocean. Like the great explorers of any age, Alexander constantly attempted to make connections between the new knowledge he gained as a result of his experiences and that which he had already possessed. (It should be mentioned that Alexander was one of the best-educated men of his day; as a youth, his tutors had included the philosopher Aristotle.) He wondered now whether the Indian Ocean was connected to the Persian Gulf; to find out, he assigned one of his officers, a Cretan named Nearchus, to return to Persia by sea. While Alexander led the rest of the army overland through the inhospitable deserts of southern Afghanistan and Iran, Nearchus captained a fleet that sailed west along the coast.

A detail from a European map of the Middle Ages depicting some of the monstrous denizens of the deep that Europeans believed could be found in the waters surrounding their continent. Until the Renaissance, Europeans rarely made long open-sea voyages, and the European collective imagination populated the ocean and the unknown realms of the globe with a host of imaginary horrors.

Alexander's march was brutal, but Nearchus's voyage was far from a pleasure cruise. Although as a native of the island of Crete Nearchus probably had some experience as a sailor, he was now in unknown waters. The tides and gales of the Indian Ocean came as an unwelcome revelation to sailors who were accustomed to the relatively placid Mediterranean Sea, and the fleet suffered several shipwrecks. The Greeks encountered other unfamiliar challenges as well: One day they saw huge jets of water shooting into the air from the surface of the sea, and moments later they were dismayed at the sight of sea monsters dead ahead. These monsters were whales, which the Mediterranean seamen had never seen before; to the Greeks, the giant mammals appeared to be huge, probably ferocious, fish. Nearchus ordered the men to bang on their drums and blow their horns as if they were going into battle. As the Greek ships advanced, making the loudest din possible, the whales disappeared beneath the surface. Moments later, the sailors looked back and saw them once more spouting on the surface, far to the rear.

For the most part, Nearchus ordered his fleet to hug the coastline. This was the common maritime practice of the day, not least because it made easier frequent resupplying of the ships. (It was not until after the epic voyages of the Portuguese sailors Bartholomeu Dias and Vasco da Gama and the Spanish explorer Christopher Columbus at the end of the 15th century that open sea voyages became commonplace.) But when Nearchus's men landed to search for food, they found the regions along the coast to be barren and uninviting. The inhabitants subsisted almost entirely on fish; even their cattle and sheep ate fish meal. Yet even this unappetizing sustenance was so scarce that the Greeks had to fight the natives for it. Starvation and illness finally made shipboard conditions so bad that Nearchus was forced to forbid his men to go ashore for fear that they would desert. At last, near Hormuz, at the narrow mouth of the Persian Gulf, Nearchus was reunited with

Alexander and the rest of the army. With fresh supplies, Nearchus then sailed the fleet up the Persian Gulf to Susa, at the mouth of the Tigris and Euphrates rivers. When Alexander arrived there later in 324, it marked the end of the emperor's great eastern expedition—the first such venture by which the people of the Mediterranean world received firsthand information about the lands between the Levant and India.

At the same time that Europe was manifesting an interest in the East, Asia was displaying curiosity about the lands to its west. Beginning in 138 B.C., Chang Ch'ien, an official of the Han dynasty in China, made several remarkable journeys across central Asia. His mission was to forge an alliance between the Chinese and the Scythians (a horse-breeding people who then inhabited Bactria) against the Hsiung-nu, or Huns, warlike, nomadic tribesmen who were migrating outward from their homeland, the steppes of northern Russia. Chang Ch'ien's mission was unsuccessful; he was captured by the Huns and remained their prisoner for more than a decade. Eventually he escaped and made his way across the Takla Makan, a desert in what is today western China. After finally reaching Scythia, he visited the region called Ferghana and the city of Kokand, which were famed for their fine horses, and he helped establish a trade arrangement whereby the Chinese bartered gold and silver for the Scythian steeds. On his way back to China he was seized by the Huns a second time. He managed to escape again, however, and he brought back to China with him information about the Gobi and Takla Makan deserts, the oases along the caravan routes, and the peoples of central Asia. He returned also with rumors of empires still farther west, beyond the land of the Scythians—of Persia, which was then called Parthia, and even of Rome—and his journey opened the door to more contacts between East and West. Beginning in about 110 B.C., China and Parthia exchanged ambassadors. The Parthian ambassador to China brought with him a

飛寒沙莽莽無南北

之霜霰風土蕭條近胡國萬里重陰烏不

腥羶豈似人狄狼喜怒難姑息行盡天山

馬上將余向絕域殄生求死死不得戎羯

第二拍

troupe of acrobats or jugglers from a place that the Chinese archives call Li-chien; they are thought to have been from the Roman Empire, perhaps from Syria. If so, they were the first Westerners to reach China.

From this time on, and for many centuries, contact between the East and the West increased steadily. Trade, travel, conquest, and diplomacy took place along two routes that connected—one by sea and one by land—eastern Asia and the Mediterranean world. In his day Marco Polo would travel both of them.

The sea route crisscrossed the Indian Ocean, from the Red Sea and the Persian Gulf in the west to the Bay of Bengal, the Java Sea, and the South China Sea in the east. The seagoing merchants who plied these waters knew how to harness the Indian Ocean's characteristic pattern of monsoon winds that change direction twice each year. Because these winds made long commercial voyages across the Indian Ocean possible, they were called trade winds.

The art of sailing across the Indian Ocean on the trade winds was pioneered by Indian sailors several thousand years ago. One such sailor, shipwrecked on the shores of

This painting on a silk scroll from the Ming dynasty depicts the abduction of a Chinese princess by the Hsiung-nu, as the Chinese referred to the Huns. The Huns were nomadic horsemen from north-central Asia whose depredations were in large part responsible for the decision of China's emperors to build the Great Wall.

the Red Sea in the 2nd century B.C., fell into the hands of Greeks who were living there and offered to show them how to sail across the Arabian Sea—the northwestern part of the Indian Ocean—to India. A Greek named Eudoxus accompanied the Indian on his homeward voyage and later returned safely; his trip opened the way for regular sea trade between the Red Sea region and India. A century later, this western end of the Indian Ocean trade was dominated by Egyptian, Greek, Syrian, and Arab mariners, many of whom were based in Alexandria, Aden (at the mouth of the Red Sea), Hormuz, Susa, and Socotra (an island off the Horn of Africa, as that continent's easternmost cape is known). Ships from these and other ports set sail for cities on the west coast of India, called the Malabar Coast, and also for the large island of Taprobane, later known as Ceylon (today it is called Sri Lanka), off the southern tip of the Indian subcontinent.

One Greek merchant sailor of the 1st century B.C. left a fascinating record of the sea trade of his era. His name and the details of his life are lost to history, but a handbook he wrote has survived. It is called the *Periplus of the Erythraean Sea* (Handbook of the Arabian Sea), and it describes the ports and sailing routes along the Egyptian, Arabian, and Persian coasts. The *Periplus* also contains information about the coast of East Africa, where considerable trade was carried on by the Indians and the Arabs, and about the ports of India, from the Malabar Coast around the southern tip and up the east coast to the mouth of the Ganges River—although the author's knowledge of these easterly regions is scanty and based mostly on hearsay. At any rate, the *Periplus* demonstrates that three centuries after Nearchus's voyage, the waters of the western Indian Ocean had become familiar territory to the people of the Mediterranean. Furthermore, it gives a vivid picture of the trade—in spices, cloth, ivory, gold and precious stones, and slaves—that flourished on both sides of the Arabian Sea.

The eastern end of the Indian Ocean trade, between India and China, was largely carried on by Indian and Malayan merchant sailors, who sailed back and forth between the east coast of India, called the Coromandel Coast, and various ports in Burma (present-day Myanmar), Malaya, Sumatra, Java, Annam (present-day Vietnam), and China, which was then called Sinae in the south and Seres in the north. Although some trade took place at the Chinese ports that are now called Guangzhong (formerly known in the English-speaking world as Canton) and Fuzhou, much of China's commerce with the outside world took place in Annam, which China controlled. Chiao Chih, or Cattigara, on the site where Hanoi now stands, was one of the busiest ports of the region, known even to Westerners. In the 2nd century A.D., a band of merchants and envoys who claimed to represent Emperor Aurelius Antoninus of Rome appeared in Cattigara. Chinese records also show that around the same time one trader from the Roman Empire—probably a Syrian—ventured north from Cattigara all the way to the capital of the emperor of China, which was then located at Chang'an (present-day Xian). The Syrian described the Mediterranean world to the Chinese emperor, who presented him with a gift of some dwarfs and sent him home.

The cultures of the Mediterranean Sea, India, and Asia were thus connected by sea. But the ocean passage, often called the Spice Route, was long, perilous, and expensive, and as a result, many merchants were reluctant to entrust their fortunes to the water. Instead, they chose the alternative, the land route from the eastern Mediterranean across the vast expanse of Eurasia to China. This route was called the Silk Road, after the precious cloth that was the driving force of East-West trade.

Silk was manufactured in China, woven from the threads spun by silkworms, which feed upon the leaves of the mulberry tree. In ancient times, the secret of sericulture, or silk manufacture, was known only to the Chinese,

Workers spin silk fiber into cloth. The West's desire for the soft, lustrous, supple cloth was perhaps the primary stimulus to trade between Europe and Asia in the centuries before the Great Interruption of geographic knowledge.

who were so determined to guard this knowledge that the penalty for smuggling a silkworm out of China was death. Silk served as a form of money in China and also was greatly desired by China's trading partners, including the Indians, the Scythians, and the Parthians. It was from trading centers in these countries, not directly from China itself, that silk made its way into the Mediterranean world.

One account drawn from ancient records says that the Roman Empire first encountered silk in 53 B.C., when the Romans fought a Parthian army at Carrhae, not far from the Euphrates River. The Parthians unfurled banners of some glistening, iridescent fabric that dazzled the Roman legions, who retreated in dismay. From that time on, the Roman Empire hungered for silk. Although this dramatic legend may be an accurate account of the first time Romans saw silk in use, they had probably heard of it earlier from the Greeks. Certainly silk had begun to enter the ports at the western end of the Spice Route by the time the *Periplus* was written. Soon it was being sold in the bazaars of Byzantium (present-day Istanbul, in Turkey) and the marketplaces of Rome. The very wealthy wore whole garments made of silk, and most people added strips of brightly dyed silk as fashionable decorations to their woolen or linen clothing. By early in the 1st century A.D., the wearing of silk had become so widespread among the well-to-do people of Rome that the Emperor Tiberius forbade men to wear it, fearing that such luxurious clothing would turn them into fops and weaklings. Around the same time, the Roman writer Pliny the Elder criticized Rome's growing taste for the exotic products of the East, especially perfumes, spices, and above all, silk. He complained that Rome sent 50 million sesterces (silver coins) eastward every year in trade for these useless luxuries.

The trade in silk had indeed become well established. Some silk reached the West by sea. It was brought from China to India either overland through Burma or by sea around Southeast Asia and Malaya; then it was shipped to ports on the Persian Gulf or the Red Sea and carried overland to Alexandria, Antioch (in Syria), or Byzantium. But most silk came to the West by the long caravan route that came to be called the Silk Road.

Just as the Spice Route consisted of a network of interconnected sea lanes, the Silk Road was not a single highway. Instead, it was a network of caravan tracks, roads, and mountain passes that stretched from one end of the Eurasian landmass to the other. A traveler or merchant on the Silk Road could choose among several main routes. One branch of the road ran from Syria or Byzantium north of the Black Sea, across the Don and Volga rivers and the steppes of what is now Russia, and north of Lake Balkhash through southern Siberia to a region called Dzungaria, which lies just south of the Altai Mountains of Mongolia. Upon emerging from Dzungaria, this northerly branch of the Silk Road merged with the larger, more traveled southern route, which is the one that Marco Polo was to immortalize in the account of his travels. It ran from the

A trade caravan files along a narrow mountain pass on the route to Antioch, an important trading center on the Silk Road. Antioch was one of the cities at the eastern end of the Mediterranean where European traders came to obtain goods from the Far East.

The legendary central Asian city of Samarkand was an important stop on the Silk Road. During its long history—it is generally regarded as the oldest city in central Asia—Samarkand has fallen under the sway of many masters, including Alexander the Great, Arab Muslims, and the Mongols.

Mediterranean coast through Mesopotamia and Persia to the city of Balkh in Bactria, the gateway to central Asia.

Balkh was located in a fertile, well-watered region between two grim mountain ranges that guard the way east: the Pamirs on the northeast and the Hindu Kush on the southeast. (The Chinese called these ranges the Lesser and Greater Headache Mountains because of the altitude sickness they induced.) At Balkh, caravans of horses and camels rested while the merchants bargained and the drivers idled away the time in the travelers' inns known as caravansaries. Whether they had come from the East or the West, many traders went no farther along the road than Balkh, for it was the crossroads where almost all travelers along the Silk Road met. Somewhere not far from Balkh, probably in Bactria or Ferghana, was a place called Tashkurgan, or Stone Tower; apparently it was named for a tall crag or mountain peak in its vicinity. Pliny the Elder wrote that the Stone Tower was the first place where merchants from China, India, Bactria, and Parthia met to barter silk and other goods. Modern scholars are still trying to determine which of the many Tashkurgans in that part of the world was Pliny's Stone Tower.

East of Balkh, the Silk Road wound its way through or around the deserts and mountains of a large region that is now divided among Afghanistan, the Asian republics of the Soviet Union, and western China. One branch of the road passed northeast from Balkh through the oasis cities of Bukhara, Samarkand, Tashkent, and Kokand and then entered Ferghana; from there it skirted the northern fringes of the Tien Shan Mountains and the Takla Makan to reach the cities of Dunhuang and Anxi, the westernmost outposts of the Chinese Empire. Another, more southerly branch of the road bore east from Balkh through a string of cities that flourished in oases along the southern edge of the Takla Makan: Kashgar, Yarkand, Khotan, and Charchan. This route, too, entered China by way of Dunhuang and Anxi.

The Silk Road thus consisted of several principal east-west routes. There were passes and connections between these routes at various points and also connections to major north-south byways. From Balkh, for example, a caravan could follow a well-traveled route that led southeast through what is now Kabul in Afghanistan and across the Khyber Pass into western India. Another route, used mainly by the Chinese and Tibetans, led south from Anxi across the desolate Tibetan plateau to the city of Lhasa and then over the Himalayas and down into eastern India and Burma. The many stages and spurs of the Silk Road were controlled by many different powers: the Romans or Persians in the west, the Chinese in the east, and between them a host of central Asian peoples and states. (In the 1st and 2nd centuries A.D. the chief power in central Asia was the Kushans, who were the descendants of the Scythians and the Greeks left in Bactria by Alexander. Later, portions of the Silk Road trade fell under the control of the Sogdians, whose capital was Samarkand; various Turkish peoples; and the Khwarazms, who lived on the southern side of the Aral Sea.) Most of the Silk Road ran through desolate and uninhabited terrain, and along the way travelers were harassed by Afghan, Indian, Turkish, and Hun bandits, who forced them to pay tolls or bribes and sometimes robbed and killed them. Most travelers—especially merchants with valuable cargoes—banded together for protection and often hired guards or mercenary soldiers to accompany them; some caravans consisted of 1,000 or more horses or camels. It was extremely rare for a traveler or caravan to attempt to cover the entire route; instead, goods were bartered or sold at various points along the way and reached the East or the West after passing through many hands.

Merchandise, of course, was not the only thing that was carried along the Silk Road; in the long run, cultural exchange would prove to be as important as commercial intercourse. Languages and customs were spread by the people of different cultures who met and traded on the trail and in the oases. Religions also traveled the Silk Road—notably Buddhism, which was carried through central Asia by wandering Buddhist pilgrims and monks from China on their way to and from sacred sites in India. One such monk was Fa-Hsien, who visited Kashgar in the 5th century B.C. and met Buddhists from many lands there. Another Buddhist monk celebrated for his travels was Hsüan-tsang, who left China in the early 7th century A.D. to "travel in the countries of the west in order to question the wise men on the points that were troubling his mind," as Chinese annals record. Hsüan-tsang covered much of the same territory that Marco Polo was to traverse 600 years later, although he was traveling in the opposite direction. He started to cross the Takla Makan, then, fearful of attack by raiding Turks, headed into the high Tien Shan range, which he described as a place where "from the beginning of the world the snow has accumulated." The monk visited Sogdiana and spent some time at Samarkand;

A caravan makes its way across the vast desert in this detail from the Catalan Atlas, *a map of the world made for the king of the Spanish province of Aragon in the 14th century. Those who traveled the Silk Road usually did so in large groups in order to discourage bandits.*

then he crossed the Pamir Mountains through a pass that was called the Iron Gate because the rocks with which it was walled were filled with iron—and also, claimed Hsüan-tsang, because a huge iron door stood at the entrance to the pass, covered with many tiny bells that rang to warn the Turks who guarded the pass when anyone tried to enter. Once across the Pamirs, Hsüan-tsang visited Balkh before heading south to India, where he spent 15 years traveling up and down the subcontinent along roads revered by Buddhists because the Buddha himself was said to have walked them. He returned north over the Hindu Kush to Yarkand, on the most southern branch of the Silk Road, and then passed through the Takla Makan with a large caravan. Upon returning to China after a 16-year absence, Hsüan-tsang found himself welcomed as a hero, and the streets of Chang'an were thronged with people eager to set eyes on the wanderer. The emperor listened eagerly to Hsüan-tsang's account of his travels, which was carefully recorded by court scribes. Under the T'ang dynasty, which came to power in China in the 7th century, China was busy expanding its borders both westward and southward, and geographic information was prized as an aid to conquest.

Additional knowledge was gained from outsiders, who were welcomed in T'ang China. Scholars, monks, traders, and wandering troupes of acrobats or magicians from Korea, Tibet, Japan, India, and Annam mingled in Chinese cities, where they met Bactrians and even Syrians from the edges of the European world. Beginning in the 7th century, many Syrian Christians migrated to central Asia and China to escape religious persecution by Roman and Byzantine Christians, who regarded them as heretics. These Nestorians, as they were called, founded Christian monasteries and communities in out-of-the-way parts of Eurasia that have survived until the present day.

Although the eastern end of the Silk Road remained fairly lively, activity on the western end declined after the

The forces of the French king, Louis IX, attack a Saracen stronghold. Louis led two crusades against the Muslims, for which he was canonized. The Crusades revitalized the practice of making pilgrimages to the Holy Land; many of the great travelers of the Middle Ages were pilgrims.

3rd century and dropped off even more sharply in the 5th century, when Rome fell to the Germanic tribes. By the 6th century, the Eastern Roman Empire (based in Byzantium, which was renamed Constantinople) and Persia had learned the secret of sericulture and were producing their own silk, although such rare Chinese silk as did make its way across the continent was still regarded as the finest. From the 7th century on, contact between the East and the West along both the Silk Road and the Spice Route was further diminished by the rise of Islam on the Arabian Peninsula. This vigorous new faith swiftly spread to Egypt, Palestine, Syria, Turkey (except for the region near the Caspian Sea called Armenia, which remained Christian), Mesopotamia, Persia, and large sections of central Asia. Before long, most of the Silk Road between Constantinople and China was in Muslim hands. As Christians and Muslims generally regarded one another as heretics and infidels, and as each faith warred against the other for converts and power, commerce, which depends on amicable relations, dwindled.

By this time, however, the countries of the West were too poor and too preoccupied with internal affairs to be much involved in trade with the East. A little commerce still took place, mostly through the efforts of Syrian, Jewish, and Greek traders who obtained goods from Alexandria and the Red Sea ports, but in general the West found itself cut off from the East. In Europe, for various reasons, geographic knowledge that had been familiar to the Greeks and Romans of the ancient world was lost, and a worldview based on Christian dogma took its place. The medieval European worldview required that all areas of knowledge conform to Christian theology, and geography was no exception. While the Arabs and the Chinese were developing systems of mapmaking and were preserving and expanding their knowledge of the world, Europeans of the Dark Ages drew maps that were based more on the Bible and on legends than on an accurate conception of physical geography. Such maps showed the Garden of Eden, the four rivers of paradise, the lands of the evil giants Gog and Magog, and other biblical features; they often placed the holy city of Jerusalem at the center of the world. The average European of the year 900, therefore, had a less accurate and less extensive notion of the world than his counterpart in 250 had possessed. The historian Daniel Boorstin has characterized this phenomenon in the development of European thought as the Great Interruption of geographic knowledge.

The rise of Islam had helped create a wall between Europe and Asia, but that barrier began to give way in 1095, when the European nations launched the first of a series of wars in the Middle East. These Crusades, as they were called, were intended to free the Holy Land where Christ was born from the Saracens, or Muslims, and also to annex some valuable territory east of the Mediterranean. The Crusades lasted into the 14th century, but although the Europeans gained some early footholds in Syria and Palestine, they were not notably successful, and the Saracens eventually regained control of the entire region.

The Crusades did, however, establish a European presence in western Asia. Cities such as Jerusalem, Antioch, and Acre fell into European hands for long periods. Equally important was the revival, as a result of the Crusades, of the practice of making pilgrimages to the Holy Land. As Europeans, for whatever reason, began to return to the Middle East, the western end of the Silk Road trade revived somewhat, and once again the people of Europe began to take notice of the East. In the 12th century, spices and other Asian goods began to trickle westward through Constantinople and Antioch, reaching Western markets mainly through the Italian merchant cities of Venice, Genoa, and Pisa. But Europe's new knowledge of Asia remained limited, for the most part, to the Levant. East of the Levant, Asia stretched away into an unknown distance, peopled with who knew what monsters and marvels.

The New Masters of Asia

For most of its long history, the Silk Road was controlled by a host of different powers that were often at war with one another, disrupting trade and travel. But in the 13th century, a new force arose in northern Asia that was to bring the entire overland route, from eastern Europe and the Levant to the Pacific coast of China, under a single ruler. That force became the Mongol Empire—the largest land empire ever known.

The Mongols were a confederation of tribes related to the Huns. Their home was the sweeping, grass-covered steppeland between Siberia and northwestern China that is today the independent nation known as the People's Republic of Mongolia. For a thousand years or more, nomadic clans of Mongols roamed the steppes with their herds of camels and horses. Their kings, called *khans*, were elected by the clan leaders at assemblies called *khur-iltais*, which were traditionally held at a sacred site on the plain of Karakorum in northern Mongolia. Occasionally, groups of Mongols migrated from their homeland to settle in other parts of Asia; the Khitans, for example, were a Mongol people who took over a portion of northern China in the 10th century. (The Turkish form of their tribal name, Khitai, was the source of the name Cathay, which was used for centuries in the West to refer to China.) For the most part, however, the Mongols remained on the steppes, out of the mainstream of history, until 1206. In that year, a brilliant and ambitious man came to power

A Mongol archer. At its height in the mid-13th century, the Mongol Empire stretched from the China Sea to the Dnieper River in western Russia, and virtually all of Europe lived in terror of attack by the dreaded Mongol horsemen.

A khuriltai *in session at the traditional Mongol capital of Karakorum. A khuriltai was the gathering of the Mongol tribal chieftains to elect a new emperor, or* khan. *Khubilai's accession to the Mongol throne was accompanied by much plotting and intrigue against him, but, Marco Polo wrote, "you must know that it was properly his by right."*

among them. His name was Temujin, which means "iron" in the Mongol language, but upon becoming the leader of all the Mongols he took the title Chinggis Khan, or "world-encompassing king." (His title is sometimes transliterated as Genghis Khan.) Under his leadership, the Mongols set out at once to live up to this title. As Marco Polo was later to put it, "They made up their minds to conquer the whole world."

The tough, highly trained Mongol horsemen and archers succeeded in conquering quite a lot of it. By 1215, Chinggis had defeated the Ch'in Empire of northern China and sacked its capital, which stood on the site of present-day Beijing. He then turned west and established dominion over two Turkish peoples, the Uighurs and the Karakhitai, who lived south of Lake Balkhash. These conquests gave him control of the eastern portion of the Silk Road, as far west as the city of Tashkent. His next target was the Islamic empire of the Khwarazms, who controlled the area between the Aral and Caspian seas as well as Persia and Afghanistan, which together constituted the west-central portion of the Silk Road. Gifted horsemen and archers, the Mongols were fierce and irresistible fighters, and although they spared cities and countries that surrendered to them, they were merciless to all who resisted: Bukhara and Samarkand were sacked, for example, and most of their inhabitants were slaughtered. By 1223, when Chinggis once more turned his armies eastward, Khwarazm was in Mongol hands. As he returned to Mongolia across the Russian steppes, Chinggis made war on the rebellious Hsi-Hsia, a people of mixed Chinese and Tibetan ancestry and culture who lived in western China. This campaign proved to be his last. After his death in 1227, his far-flung empire was divided into territories called khanates, each ruled by one of his descendants. Chinggis's grandson Batu was named Khan of the Golden Horde, the westernmost of the khanates, located near the Caspian and Aral seas. Chinggis's son Chaghadai received central Asia, from the Aral Sea to the western edge of China. Another son, Tolui, was given the Mongol homeland. A third son, Ögödei, was named khan of China and also *khaghan* (khan of khans, or Great Khan), with overlordship of the entire empire. A fifth khanate was added when Hulegu, Tolui's son, completed the Mongol conquest of Persia, Mesopotamia, and Syria; he was given these lands to rule and founded the Il-Khanid Dynasty in Persia.

News of the Mongol expansion traveled westward ahead of the horde itself, and some people in Christian Europe began to hope that the Mongols might serve as their allies by destroying the Saracens, but Ögödei dispelled these hopes with a renewed Mongol assault on the West. In 1240, Batu's Golden Horde seized and sacked the city of Kiev, in southern Russia. Other Russian cities followed, and a contemporary account of the Mongol onslaught at Ryazan provides graphic testimony to their fury: "The inhabitants, without regard to age or sex, were slaughtered with the savage cruelty of Mongol revenge; some were impaled, some shot at with arrows for sport, others were flayed or had nails or splinters driven under their nails. Priests were roasted alive, and nuns and maidens ravished in the churches before their relatives. No eye remained open to weep for the dead." The next year, Mongol armies advanced into eastern Europe. They routed the defenders of Poland and Hungary and laid waste to these countries, killing many of their inhabitants. All of Europe quaked with fear; the invaders from the East seemed invincible. The Mongols were poised on the borders of Austria and southern Germany, ready to march into the heart of the West, when Europe received what its inhabitants regarded as a miraculous reprieve. The Mongol war leaders received word from Karakorum that Ögödei, the Great Khan, was dead. The khans abandoned their assault on Europe and hastened back to Karakorum to attend the khuriltai at which his successor would be chosen. *(continued on page 42)*

The Legend of Prester John

To Europeans at the time of the Crusades, Asia was a vast *terra incognita*, or unknown land, a map whose blank spaces could be filled in with imagination or fable. One fable that captured the imaginations of Europeans was the legend of Prester John, a Christian king who was said to dwell somewhere in the dim regions of the East. Not only was Prester John fabulously wealthy, or so the story ran; he was also the commander of a mighty army that would someday come to the aid of the beleaguered Christians who were fighting the Saracens in the Holy Land.

The title *prester* is a version of presbyter, which means "priest," and John was believed to be both a monarch and a priest. He was first mentioned in the writings of one Otto, a German bishop, who wrote that in 1145 he had met a Syrian bishop who had told him all about a Christian king named John who lived somewhere beyond Persia. According to Otto, this John had tried to come to Jerusalem to fight on the side of the Christian Crusaders, but he had been unable to find a way to get his army across the Tigris River, and so, after hanging about on the riverbank for a few years, was "obliged to return home." Despite what some might have seen as a disappointing lack of resourcefulness on Prester John's part in regard to the river crossing, the people of Europe were cheered to think of a potential ally somewhere out there on the far side of the Saracen lands—an ally who might soon smite the Muslim forces in the rear. But Prester John was not heard of again until about 1165, at which time a letter, allegedly penned by John himself, began circulating through the courts and cities of Europe. About 10 pages in length, it consisted mostly of boasts about Prester John's high rank, his wealth, and his godliness.

Prester John claimed to rule over 72 kings and their kingdoms; in fact, he was so far above ordinary rulers that even his cook and his butler were kings. His realm contained the Tower of Babel, the Fountain of Youth, a river of gems, a race of centaurs, a land of warrior women, and many other wonders. It was not, however, home to any poor people, liars, thieves, or sinners. Prester John owned heaps of gold and jewels, and in front of his palace stood a magic mirror in which he could view all parts of his dominion. He was a mighty war leader, a just and powerful ruler, and the greatest monarch under Heaven—and, of course, he was more humble than any other Christian.

All of this was immensely fascinating to the West. Prester John's letter was translated into a dozen or more European languages, and hundreds of copies of it were passed from hand to hand. In 1177, Pope Alexander III wrote back to Prester John; several copies of his letter have been preserved, but none bears an address, for even the pope had to admit that he had no idea where to find the mysterious and powerful Christian monarch. In the absence of facts, the mapmakers and geographers of the period made do with guesses. At first, most of them placed Prester John's kingdom somewhere in India, possibly through confusion with the apostle St. Thomas, who had died in India. Later, Prester John's realm was thought to lie somewhere in the uncharted heart of central Asia, a belief that may have been based on the existence of Nestorian and Armenian Christian communities in those parts. By the 14th century, most European geographers had given up on Asia and were optimistically placing

Prester John in the African kingdom of Abyssinia, or Ethiopia, which was in fact ruled by Christians. As late as the end of the 16th century, Prester John's realm still appeared on some Dutch and German maps of southern or eastern Africa.

Scholars have never determined who wrote the letter of 1165, and Prester John's kingdom, like the legendary golden city of el Dorado in the Americas, was never found. But like el Dorado, it was a chimera, a shimmering illusion, that inspired many explorers and adventurers. The epic Portuguese sea voyages around Africa to India and beyond in the 15th and 16th centuries were motivated in part by the still widespread belief that a mighty Christian nation—Prester John's kingdom—waited to be discovered somewhere in the East.

Prester John as he appeared in a woodcut illustrating the title page of a 1495 Italian manuscript entitled Treatise on the Supreme Prester John.

(continued from page 39)

In their absence, the rulers of Europe debated how to meet the Mongol threat. (Most Europeans referred to the Mongols as Tartars, after a branch of the Mongol people who were called Tatars, from the Chinese word *ta-ta*, which means "nomad." Europeans confused the name Tatar with Tartarus, an ancient Greek name for hell, which—in view of the Mongols' ferocity—seemed like an appropriate home for them, and called them Tartars and their central Asian territory Tartary.) Pope Gregory IX called for a Christian crusade against the Mongols, but no one rallied to his cry. In 1245, his successor, Pope Innocent IV, convened a special council in Lyons, France, for the purpose of "finding a remedy for the Tartars and other spurners of the faith and persecutors of the people of Christ." This learned gathering "advised, besought, and entreated all Christian people to block every road or passage by which the enemy could pass, either by means of ditches, walls, buildings and other contrivances."

By this time, the Muslims of Persia and the Levant had lost even more lives and more territory to the Mongols than had Christian Europe. In desperation, they sent their own envoys to Lyons, begging their longtime foes, the Christian leaders of Europe, to unite with them against the nomadic hordes. To their dismay, some Christian rulers speculated that it might be possible to form an alliance with the Tartars against the Saracens. Most Europeans, however, scorned the idea of joining with either the Saracens or the Tartars. The bishop of Winchester, England, summed up the general reaction: "Let dog bite dog," he said, expressing the pious hope that the Tartars and Saracens would destroy one another and leave Europe in peace.

Pope Innocent was among those who believed that perhaps the Tartars were the lesser of the two evils. The Saracens, after all, were Muslims, but the Tartars were only heathens. If they could be converted to Christianity, then Europe would be safe from their onslaught and the

West would have a worthy ally against Islam. Desiring to learn more about the Mongols, the pope sent an envoy to them. This messenger's name was Giovanni di Plano Carpini (in English, John of Plano Carpini). He became the first European in many centuries to have crossed Asia, and his journey launched a new era in Western travel to the East.

Carpini was born sometime around 1180 near Perugia, Italy. A friend and disciple of St. Francis of Assisi, he became a friar, or monk, of the Franciscan order of the Roman Catholic church and taught and preached in Germany, Spain, and France. When he was selected by the pope to be Europe's first formal emissary to the Tartars, he was more than 60 years old.

A Persian depiction of the Mongol sack of Baghdad. The Mongol armies were most feared for the speed and mobility of their horsed warriors, but in order to conquer the cities of Asia and the Middle East they were also forced to become adept at siege warfare.

Carpini set off eastward on Easter Sunday in April 1245, accompanied by a fellow friar, Stephen of Bohemia. While traveling through Poland they were joined by a third friar, Benedict the Pole, who spoke some Mongol and was to serve as their interpreter. Upon entering Batu's Russian territory they frequently encountered the grim signs of the Mongol conquest: deserted villages and cities devastated by fire and war. At Kiev, on the Dnieper River, the destruction convinced Friar Stephen to go no farther. In early February 1246, Carpini left him behind and forged ahead across the great rivers of southern Russia—the Dnieper, the Don, and the Volga. In April he and Benedict

A mounted Mongol archer. Mongol ponies were small but remarkably hardy; each warrior had anywhere from 3 to 20 at his disposal while on the march. The Mongols' skill with the bow and arrow and the mobility given them by their horsemanship enabled them to avoid much of the deadly hand-to-hand combat of the day, and Christian Europe feared them as the "Scourge of God."

arrived on the far bank of the Volga River, where stood Batu's *ordu*, or tent camp (the source of the English word *horde*). Before Carpini and Benedict could be presented to Batu Khan, they had to walk between two blazing fires. Having completed this ceremony, they presented gifts and greetings to Batu, who told them that it was necessary for them to deliver their message to Karakorum, the heart of the Mongol Empire. The Franciscans agreed willingly, the Mongols provided them with transportation for the journey eastward, and the monks set forth on the second leg of their journey on April 8, 1246, another Easter Sunday.

Every traveler in the Mongol domains was to admire the rapid, efficient transportation and mail system with which the Mongols held together their sprawling empire. Carpini was the first Westerner to visit the many post stations that the Mongols had built along the northern route of the Silk Road, across Russia and southern Siberia. These stations had been placed close enough together that a rider could change horses 5 or 6 times in a day; an imperial messenger, covering 250 miles or more a day on fresh horses, could ride from one end of the empire to the other in a couple of weeks. (The road was also frequently patrolled by the Mongol cavalry and local militias, which helped to ensure the safety of travelers and reduce the prevalence of banditry.) Carpini and his companions did not travel quite so rapidly, but they set a fast pace, carried in carts drawn by sturdy Mongol horses that could plow through the snow of the mountain passes and forage on the scanty grass of Dzungaria and the Gobi Desert. Early each morning the Europeans were roused by their Mongol escorts, who wrapped them tightly in strips of cloth to prevent them from being injured by the rough, jolting ride, placed them in their carts, and drove them over the plains on rutted roads until nightfall. Carpini, who was ill at the time and greatly overweight to boot, found the journey miserably uncomfortable.

As the party passed north of the Caspian and Aral seas, crossed the Ural River, and passed Tashkent and other Muslim cities, Carpini glimpsed the havoc that the Mongols had wrought during their conquest of central Asia. At last, after crossing the snow-clad Altai Mountains and skirting the northern fringes of the Gobi, the party reached Karakorum in late July. Carpini and fellow travelers had covered the distance from the Volga to Karakorum—more than 3,000 miles—in 106 days.

Karakorum was a campground, not a city, although some buildings and monasteries were eventually built there by later Mongol leaders. In Carpini's time, it was still a vast, empty plain upon which the various khans pitched their tents and pastured their horses. At the center of this array was Sira Orda (Yellow Pavilion), the imperial Mongol camp. Carpini was amazed by both the size and the diversity of the gathering at Karakorum. He had arrived at a crucial time, for Ögödei's son and successor, Guyug, was about to be confirmed as the Great Khan. The event was attended by more than 3,000 envoys from all parts of the Mongol Empire: Manchurians (from the northeast-ernmost part of China, on the border with Siberia), Chinese, Tibetans, Khwarazms, Persians, and others, as well as representatives from all the khanates and branches of the Mongol confederacy. Although he was disappointed to find no trace of Prester John, the legendary Christian monarch of Asia, Carpini was impressed by the breadth and scope of the Mongol world. He also noted with admiration that the Mongols, who were regarded by the Europeans as well as by the Chinese as uncouth barbarian horsemen because they built no cities of their own, adorned their tents, wagons, and horses with gold, silk, furs, and precious stones.

Carpini and Benedict were lodged in the camp of the Golden Horde. On August 24 they witnessed the formal ceremony in which Guyug became Great Khan. Guyug received costly gifts from the foreign envoys, including

500 carts filled with silk and gold, which he divided among the various khans. Soon thereafter, the Franciscans were presented to the new ruler. He asked immediately if they had any presents for him, and they had to admit rather sheepishly that they had already given away everything they had brought with them just to get this far. They did, however, give Guyug a letter from the pope, in which Innocent urged the Great Khan to apologize for the atrocities committed against Christians by the Tartars, to become a Christian himself, and to leave Europe alone. Guyug, unmoved by the pope's entreaties, dictated his own letter to Innocent. "How can We foresee what will happen to you? Heaven alone knows. . . . You must come yourself at the head of all your kings and prove to Us your fealty and allegiance. And if you disregard the command of God and disobey Our instructions, We shall look upon you as Our enemy. Whoever recognizes and submits to

Ögödei was the third son of Chinggis Khan and succeeded his father as Great Khan. Under his leadership the Mongols effectively completed their subjugation of China and conquered virtually all of Russia, thereby gaining the greatest land empire in the history of the world. Only his death in 1241 prevented the Mongols from carrying their onslaught to western Europe.

the Son of God and Lord of the World, the Great Khan, will be saved, whoever refuses submission will be wiped out," he wrote, rightly foreseeing that the effect of such a belligerent missive would be to keep the Europeans guessing about the Mongols' intentions. He then gave the Franciscans permission to depart, and they set forth from Karakorum in November. Guyug offered to send some Tartars back to Europe with them, but Carpini declined, fearing that if the Tartars saw how quarrelsome and disunified the European states were they would renew their attack.

After a brisk but rigorous winter journey across the snow-covered deserts, Carpini arrived in Kiev in June 1247 and went on to deliver the Great Khan's message to Pope Innocent at Lyons. He wrote an account of his trip that was published as *The History of the Mongols*. It discussed the geography, climate, history, customs, religions, and culture of Mongolia and central Asia, and it included a list of the peoples that had been conquered by the Tartars. Carpini's story was anxiously awaited and well received, for it was the first direct account of life among the Mongol hordes. Ultimately, he grew so tired of being asked to tell about his trip that he would instruct his listeners to read his book aloud and ask questions only if they came across something they did not understand.

One of the many people who met Carpini and heard his story was another Franciscan friar, William of Rubruck, who held a post at the court of King Louis IX of France. While leading the Seventh Crusade, Louis received information—unfortunately quite erroneous—that some of the Mongol leaders had converted to Christianity and would welcome an alliance and instruction in the tenets of Christianity. He decided to send Friar William, who was then about 38 years old and spoke Arabic and a little Mongol, to Karakorum to see what was happening in the Mongol world.

The king equipped Rubruck for his journey with a Bible, a little money, and some letters for the Great Khan; the queen added a prayer book and some church robes. He was accompanied by one Friar Bartholomew, of whom little is known save that he was a drunkard, and a couple of servants. This somewhat motley assemblage set off from Constantinople, which was temporarily in Christian hands, on May 7, 1253. By following much the same route as Carpini had taken, the Franciscan and his bibulous companion reached the headquarters of the Golden Horde, only to discover that no one there had the slightest interest in becoming a Christian. Undeterred, they pushed on to Karakorum, although the journey, despite the help of a Mongol guide, was apparently an unpleasant one. Rubruck, like Carpini, was very stout, and he complained much about the discomforts of the trip—biting cold, enervating heat, howling winds, and undercooked and nearly inedible food, which rendered the friar almost prostrate with hunger.

Rubruck and his companions arrived in Karakorum in December. They knew already that Guyug had died; now they learned that his successor was Chinggis's grandson Möngke, whom the friar described as a little man somewhat fond of intoxicating drink. Rubruck was chagrined to discover that neither the new Great Khan nor any of his subjects wished to be baptized, but he did find that unlike European rulers, Möngke Khan and the Tartars in general were quite tolerant of other religions. They allowed their subjects to practice all faiths freely; Rubruck met Buddhists, Chinese Taoists, Muslims, and Nestorian and Armenian Christians in the Mongol domain. Möngke cleverly told Rubruck that as Christians seemed unable to follow the laws of their God, such as those forbidding them to quarrel with one another, he would continue in the Mongols' ancestral faith, which involved worship of a sky spirit and ritual fortune-telling. Rather sadly, Rubruck wrote, "If I had had the power to work by signs and wonders like Moses, perhaps he would have humbled himself." Möngke's written reply to King Louis, composed, according to Rubruck, with the aid of "not infrequent consultation of the flagon at his side," was more bellicose. "This, by the virtue of the eternal, throughout the great world of the Mongols, is the message of Möngke Khan to the Lord of the French," he wrote. "Wherever ears can hear, wherever horses can travel, there let it be heard and known; these who do not believe, but resist our commandments, shall not be able to see with their eyes, or hold with their hands, or walk with their feet." (In later years, most Mongols became Buddhists, some became Muslims, and a few adopted Christianity.)

Rubruck left Karakorum in July 1254 and reached Europe about a year later. He brought with him a storehouse of information gathered along the way, including the first substantial account in the West of Buddhism and a number of facts about Cathay, or China. In Paris, he met Roger Bacon, an English monk and scientist, who listened eagerly to the story of his travels and incorporated it in an encyclopedia he published in 1268. It was through Bacon's writings that Rubruck's journey became known to educated Europeans.

The journeys of Carpini and Rubruck, which represented a renewed European interest in gaining knowledge about the East, were motivated by religious and political concerns, but after their return a new breed of traveler would arise, one driven by an even older motivation— commerce. Now that the Tartars had reduced Muslim strength in the Levant and central Asia, the way eastward from Europe seemed open once again. The Silk Road was now under the control of a single unified force: the Mongol Empire, which appeared willing to tolerate and even to protect travelers from the West. While Carpini and Rubruck were making their futile attempts to turn the Mongols

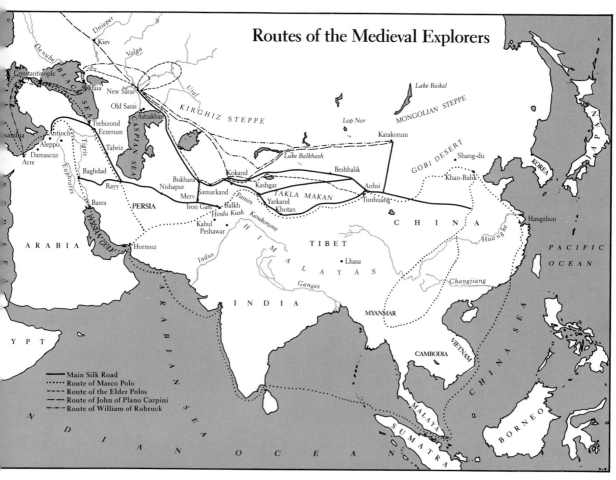

Routes of the Medieval Explorers

Main Silk Road
Route of Marco Polo
Route of the Elder Polos
Route of John of Plano Carpini
Route of William of Rubruck

into Christian allies, merchants in Europe were eyeing the Tartars as potential new trade partners. This was especially true in the great mercantile cities of the Italian coast, which had long carried on business in the Levant, in Turkey, and in the Black Sea ports of southern Russia. Around 1254 in Venice, the richest and most powerful of these cities, at about the same time that William of Rubruck was making his rugged trip home from Mongolia, a boy named Marco Polo was born into a family of merchants. Not many years later, he would help make his family the most famous travelers of all time.

Important trade roads and the routes taken by travelers during medieval times.

The Polos on the Silk Road

Not much is known about the Polo family or about Marco Polo's early life. His father, Nicolo Polo, was one of three sons of a Venetian named Andrea Polo; the other two sons were named Marco and Maffeo. It appears that the Polos were members of the minor nobility of their city-state and that the three brothers were business partners in a trading concern. The eldest, Marco, lived in Constantinople, where he looked after the family's business interests there and in Soldaia (present-day Sudak), a city on the Crimean Peninsula, across the Black Sea from Constantinople.

It is not known for certain when Nicolo's son Marco was born, although most accounts agree that it was probably in 1254. Shortly before the baby was due, Nicolo and Maffeo Polo left Venice on a trading trip to Constantinople, where they remained for the next six years. In 1260, word reached the West that a new Great Khan had been elected in the Mongol homeland. His name was Khubilai, and he was the grandson of Chinggis Khan. Khubilai's accession to power marked the beginning of a century of relative peace within the Mongol Empire and between East and West that later historians would call the Pax Mongolica or Pax Tatarica (the Peace of the Mongols). During this period, Europeans felt freer and safer than ever before to travel within the Mongol Empire.

Among the first to profit from the Pax Mongolica were Nicolo and Maffeo Polo. The brothers took a cargo of

Constantinople, the seven-hilled "second city of Christendom," was the center for the Polo brothers' trade operations in the Middle East.

gems to Soldaia, where a considerable number of Venetian
traders lived in a sort of merchant colony, and from there
ventured eastward on horseback into Mongol lands. At a
place called Sarai on the Volga River, they came upon
the encampment of Berke, who had inherited the khanate
of the Golden Horde after Batu's death. Berke bought their
gems at a generous price, gave them some gifts, and generally treated the Polos so well that they remained in Sarai
for about a year. Warfare between Berke and Hulegu, the
khan of Persia, had closed some of the western roads and
thus made impossible the Polos' planned return, by way
of Constantinople, so they went east instead, to the city
of Bukhara, near the Aral Sea. In Bukhara, where they
remained for some time—perhaps as long as three years—
they met some of Khubilai's messengers, who invited the
Venetians to visit their master. Khubilai Khan had never
met any Europeans, although he greatly wished to do so,
and the envoys assured the Polos that they would be welcome at the Great Khan's court. Because Khubilai had
just moved the Mongol capital from Karakorum to northern China, the Polo brothers were the first Westerners to
be invited to China.

They made their way across Asia, encountering, as Nicolo's son Marco was later to report, "great wonders and
a variety of things," and were hospitably received by Khubilai Khan, who questioned them eagerly about the nations
of the West and about Christianity. When the Polos ex-
pressed the desire to return home, he made them promise
to return someday, and he entrusted them with a letter to
the pope, whom he addressed as "Master the Apostle."
The missive asked the pope to send 100 learned Christian
men to China to debate the merits of Christianity with
representatives of other faiths. Khubilai also gave them a
gold tablet that guaranteed their safe passage through his
realm and required his subjects to provide them with supplies and assistance as needed. These tablets, which essentially functioned as passports for travel within the
Mongol Empire, were known as *paizahs*, which means

"tablets of command." They were about a foot long and four inches wide, often set with a gem and decorated with drawings of various animals and fowl that the Mongols regarded as sacred. A crime against the bearer of a paizah was regarded as a crime against the khan himself.

After an absence of about 15 years, Nicolo and Maffeo Polo returned to Venice in 1269. Of course, much had changed while they were gone. Nicolo discovered that his wife had died and that he had a teenage son named Marco. He and Maffeo also learned that Pope Clement IV was dead, which meant that they would have to wait until the officials of the Catholic church elected a new pope to present the pontiff with the Great Khan's letter.

The Polos waited for several years, but the election of the new pope was repeatedly delayed by political squabbling. Finally, in 1271, fearing that undue delay might anger Khubilai and damage their prospects for trade with his empire, the Polos decided they could wait no longer and set off once more for the East at the head of a caravan of trade goods and servants, accompanied this time by

Maffeo and Nicolo Polo present the newly elected pope, Gregory X, with Khubilai Khan's letter requesting that the pontiff send him 100 theological scholars with whom his own wise men could debate the merits of Christianity. The illustration is from an early 15th-century French manuscript entitled The Book of Wonders, *which contained Marco's narrative as well as the accounts of other explorers and adventurers.*

young Marco Polo. They had proceeded only a short way along the Silk Road when messengers overtook them with the news that a new pope had just been named. The Polos returned to Acre, on the Mediterranean coast, where the newly elected Pope Gregory X gave them a letter of greeting for Khubilai. The pope attempted to fill the Great Khan's request for 100 learned men, but the Catholic clergymen of Acre showed some reluctance to undertake the mission and Gregory was able to come up with only two monks of the Dominican order, Friar Nicolas of Vicenza and Friar William of Tripoli.

The Polos lost Nicolas and William in Turkey, when the two clergymen were so frightened by marauding bands of Saracens that they refused to continue, but Maffeo, Nicolo, and Marco traveled on undaunted. They had gone northeast from Acre to pass through Turkey, and their route then took them east through Armenia and southeast along the Tigris River through Baghdad, a mighty Muslim metropolis and center of learning, then southeast through Persia to the ancient port of Hormuz on the Persian Gulf. All of these lands were in Mongol hands.

Young though he was, Marco Polo was an enthusiastic and observant traveler. He paid considerable attention to the landscapes, peoples, products, and customs of the places the Polos passed through, and he also collected a great deal of information about regions that lay to either side of the Polos' route. Thus, upon his return many years later, he was able to describe not only the many fabled lands that he had visited but also to give some account of many countries and landmarks that he had not seen personally. (Although his narrative varies wildly in terms of reliability, Marco's firsthand descriptions are generally more accurate than those based on hearsay.)

Marco Polo's account of the journey east combines elements of the marvelous and the mundane. In discussing Armenia, for example, he speaks of Mount Ararat, "on which Noah's ark is said to have rested." After describing the mountain's great size and its forbiddingly icy peak, he

(continued on page 65)

A World of Wonders

A caravan continues on its way after stopping at a caravansary.

In one sense, it can be argued that Marco Polo was not really an explorer. He did not make any new geographic discoveries in the sense in which the term *discovery* is applied to the achievements of Christopher Columbus or Vasco da Gama, for example; educated Europeans, though small in number, already knew of the existence of China. He pioneered no new routes to the East; indeed, he traveled the two most well used courses connecting Europe and Asia. The intrepid Venetian was essentially an extremely ambitious business traveler, using well-traveled, albeit remote and dangerous, highways to seek out new opportunities to increase his fortune. Yet such an assessment, despite its partial accuracy, is far too simplistic and does Polo an injustice, for he possessed a quality that has made him a paragon of exploration for countless generations of travelers since his day: relentless curiosity. *Discovery* is a relative term; unless always and completely uninhabited, no land is ever truly discovered. But in a very real way, those who, like Marco Polo, succeed through a combination of gifts of intellect and perception in seeing a place as it has never been seen before are discoverers and explorers in the best sense of the words. Others had been to China before Marco and had even written of their adventures, but it was his marvelous openness to new experiences that made his unique portrayal of the wondrous East so convincing, stimulating, and timeless.

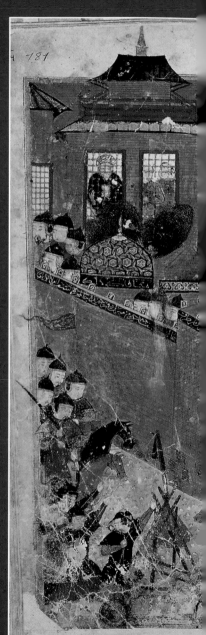

An Arab dhow. The lateen rigging used by Arab dhows, when applied to European ships known as caravels, helped make possible the great voyages of discovery of the Renaissance. East-West commercial and cultural interchange did not begin with Marco Polo, of course, but his travels and narratives were extremely important in terms of alerting Europe to the great riches and technical achievements of the non-European world.

A Persian manuscript illustrating the Mongol sack of Baghdad. A trembling Europe saw the Mongols as little more than fiendish, murderous marauders, but Marco painted quite a different picture.

This scene from an illuminated Persian manuscript shows trading vessels calling at the Port of Hormuz, on the Persian Gulf. Hormuz lay astride one of the important sea routes connecting the West and the East.

Workers pick tea on India's Malabar Coast in this illustration of a medieval French edition of Marco's book, A Description of the World. *Tea was one of the "spices" from the East that Europe craved, and it was the attempt of European mariners such as Columbus and da Gama, many of whom were influenced by the writings of Marco, to find a sea route to Asia that brought about what historians have called the first great age of discovery.*

A Ming dynasty portrait of a Mongol horseman on the move. Much attention has been focused on the more sensational, bellicose aspects of Mongol culture, but as Marco pointed out, the Mongols were also enlightened administrators and technical innovators and were tolerant of a broad spectrum of religious belief.

A trading scene, from the French
manuscript known as The Book of
Wonders. Marco's account of the fabulous
wealth of the East greatly stimulated
Europe's desire for commerce with Asia,
which ultimately resulted in the discovery
of new trade routes and the New World.

Dog-headed people were among the oddities believed by medieval Europeans to reside in the East. Although Marco's book was not totally devoid of fabrication, its overall wealth of reliable detail made it an invaluable counterweight to such preposterous beliefs.

A *humble beginning for a momentous journey:*
Marco Polo leaves his home city of Venice.
The illustration is from an English edition
of A Description of the World *published*
around 1400.

(continued from page 56)

mentions that its lower slopes are well watered and provide excellent grazing for cattle and sheep. His view of things is always, to some extent, that of the merchant—he describes each place in terms of what it produces and how the land can be used, as when he observes that a natural oil well in the province of Georgia (probably a forerunner of the oil fields of present-day Baku) produces enough oil to load 100 ships at a time and that the oil, although not good to eat, can be used for fuel or as a salve for skin irritations on men or camels. This grasp of the particular, this interest in the practical aspect of things, gives his observations a tone of shrewd reliability that balances the more exaggerated and fabulous elements of his story. He also noted carefully three subjects of perennial interest to the traveler: food, water, and accommodation. Speaking of the inhabitants of Hormuz, for example, he echoed accounts of Nearchus's much earlier voyage when he reported that the Persians of the gulf lived on dried and salted fish, onions, and dates. "The natives do not eat our sort of food," he reported, "because a diet of wheaten bread and meat would make them ill."

The Polos had gone south to Hormuz with the intention of continuing eastward from there by sea. Marco was impressed by this port city, with its excellent harbor—"Merchants come here by ship from India," he said, "bringing all sorts of spices and precious stones and pearls and cloths of silk and of gold and elephants' tusks and many other wares"—but he and the elder Polos were less taken with the quality of the Arab and Indian vessels they saw there. "Their ships are very bad," said Marco, "and many of them founder, because they are not fastened with iron nails but stitched together with a thread made of coconut husks." Unwilling to risk a long sea passage in one of these seemingly unseaworthy craft, the Polos decided to complete their journey by land, along the Silk Road.

Accordingly, they turned their steps to the north and east and crossed Persia, which Marco learned was at that time divided into eight smaller kingdoms, each of whose

"There never was a man, be he Christian or Saracen or Tartar or Heathen, who ever travelled over so much of the world as did that noble and illustrious citizen of Venice, Marco Polo," wrote his ghostwriter, Rustichello of Pisa. This portrait of Polo was done many centuries after his death; no likeness of him from life is known to exist.

principal products and characteristics he later described. Yazd, for example, was noted for a fine cloth of silk and gold produced by its weavers; Kerman, for its turquoises and for the military equipment—saddles, swords, and the like—manufactured by its craftsmen. He also reported on the Karuanas, a half-Indian, half-Mongol people of southern and eastern Persia who lived by banditry and were greatly feared by travelers. It was said that the Karuanas had mastered certain Indian "magical and diabolical arts, by means of which they are enabled to produce darkness, obscuring the light of day to such a degree that persons are invisible to one another." (Latter-day interpreters have suggested that the magical darknesses produced by the Karuanas may simply have been mountain fogs and mists.) According to Marco's book, he and his party were set upon by Karuanas and forced to take refuge in a nearby tower; they later escaped, although some members of their caravan were captured and killed or sold into slavery.

In eastern Persia, the Polos crossed the Dasht-e-Lut, a bleak desert of mingled salt and sand, then entered the fertile province of Khorasan. Like many travelers after him, Marco remarked on the excellent melons of that region, which he thought were "the best in the world." In Bactria, the Polos stopped at Balkh, which Marco described as "a large and magnificent city" that had sustained much damage from the Tartar attacks. Its marble palaces and spacious squares, he said, lay partly in ruins.

After leaving Balkh, the Polos entered Badakhshan, a region that lies in what is today the northernmost part of Afghanistan, extending into the Pamir Mountains. Badakhshan, said Marco, was inhabited by a Muslim people descended from Alexander the Great. Its principle products were lapis lazuli (a blue semiprecious stone), rubies, silver, and horses. He added that a particular breed of Badakhshan steeds was reputed to have been descended from Alexander's celebrated warhorse Bucephalus but that a few years earlier a quarrel between two princes had led to the destruction of this entire breed "and thus the race was lost to the world." Badakhshan was a cold region, observed Marco, but its pure, clear mountain air cured fevers and other illnesses; according to some versions of his story, he or someone in his party fell sick and remained in Badakhshan for a year before recovering sufficiently to go on. Marco also describes Peshawar, in Pakistan, and Kashmir, in northern India, but these descriptions are probably based on hearsay, as it is not likely that the Polos took side trips from Badakhshan to these regions. Information about them was probably obtained by the Polos from Indian and Pakistani traders whom they met at the various caravansaries where they most likely stayed at night.

East of Badakhshan, the Polos' route led them up and up through the Pamir Mountains. Marco was the first Western writer to describe this corner of Asia, which he

A caravansary was an inn surrounding a large open courtyard along the Silk Road and other routes in the Middle East. There, the weary traveler could sleep and get a meal while his animals were tended to, watered, and fed. This is a 17th-century artist's depiction of one such caravansary in Persia.

The Kirghiz herdsmen who grazed their flocks in the region referred to the Pamir Mountains as the Roof of the World. The world's 4 greatest mountain ranges converge on the Pamirs, and all but 2 of the world's 94 tallest peaks are located in the region.

thought was the highest point on earth. "No birds fly here because of the height and the cold," he said. "And I assure you that, because of this great cold, fire is not so bright here nor of the same color as elsewhere, and food does not cook well." As improbable as this assertion seemed to Marco's readers, later travelers at high altitudes confirmed that water boils more slowly on mountains than at sea level. It took the party 52 days to cross this bleak region, during which they seldom saw any living thing aside from themselves. Apart from scattered sightings of "savage, ill-disposed, and idolatrous" hunters, the only evidence of human life they encountered were cattle pens left by the nomads who brought their herds to the heights to graze in summer. These pens were constructed out of the interlaced horns of the region's wild sheep. Although Marco did not see any sheep, in later years the species would be named after him—*Ovis poli* in the Latin nomenclature of scientific classification. The horns served another purpose as well: At various points, previous travelers had heaped the bones into piles that served as eerie guideposts across the snowy, frigid range.

The crossing of the Pamirs proved to be the most desolate and uncomfortable portion of the journey east. Upon descending the eastern slopes of the mountains, the Polos found themselves on the great plain of Chinese Turkestan (today the province of Xinjiang in western China). There they stopped at the ancient trading cities along the southernmost branch of the Silk Road, including Kashgar, Yarkand, and Khotan. As always, Marco noted each city's industries: Kashgar produced cotton cloth; Yarkand featured expert craftsmen; and Khotan had many farms, vineyards, and gardens. Marco also describes Samarkand, one of the great metropolises of Turkestan, although he visited it later, during his stay in China, and not on the way to the Great Khan's court. He reported that it was a noble and beautiful city torn by strife between its Christian and Muslim inhabitants.

The marketplace at Khotan, the Silk Road city built on an oasis at the edge of the Takla Makan. The Polos stopped at Khotan, which was renowned for the fine jade work of its craftsmen and the wheat, rice, oats, maize, cotton, apricots, peaches, and apples grown by its farmers.

From Khotan, the Polos faced only one more long stretch of rough travel before they reached Khubilai Khan's court, but it was a daunting prospect indeed. They had to cross the southern part of the Gobi Desert, or the Desert of Lop, as it was sometimes called. At a city called Lop—probably located near the salty lake that is still called Lop Nor, or Lake Lop—they rested and let their tired horses eat their fill of grass. Then they embarked on the desert crossing, which took about a month. There were wells a day's distance apart but no food, so the travelers had to carry plenty of provisions. Hunger, however, was not their greatest worry; they were more afraid of the spirits that were said to haunt the desert and lure unwary travelers to their doom. These same fears had terrified Hsüan-tsang, the Buddhist monk, when he crossed the desert 600 years earlier. Marco explained:

> When a man is riding by night through this desert and
> something happens to make him loiter and lose touch with
> his companions, by dropping asleep or for some other
> reason, and afterwards he wants to rejoin them, then he
> hears spirits talking in such a way that they seem to be his
> companions. Sometimes, indeed, they even hail him by

The Takla Makan, at the southern extremity of the Gobi Desert, has terrified travelers for centuries. The Chinese called the portion of the desert that the Polos crossed the Flowing Sands because the fierce Gobi wind, called in winter the buran, *constantly rearranged the position of the dunes. More than one wayfarer believed the resulting "whispering" of the shifting sands to be the voices of spirits enticing the traveler to his doom.*

name. Often these voices make him stray from the path, so that he never finds it again. And in this way many travelers have been lost and have perished. And sometimes in the night they are conscious of a noise like the clatter of a great cavalcade of riders away from the road; and, believing that they are some of their own company, they go where they hear the noise and, when day breaks, find that they are victims of an illusion and in an awkward plight. And there are some who, in crossing this desert, have seen a host of men coming towards them and, suspecting that they were robbers, have taken flight; so, having left the beaten track and not knowing how to return to it again, they have gone hopelessly astray. Yes, and even by daylight men hear these spirit voices, and often you fancy you are listening to the strains of many instruments, especially drums, and the clash of arms. For this reason bands of travelers make a point of keeping very close together. Before they go to sleep they set up a sign pointing in the direction in which they have to travel. And round the necks of all their beasts they fasten little bells, so that by listening to the sound they may prevent them from straying off the path.

The Polos managed to cross the desert, which the Chinese called the Flowing Sands, without running afoul of any malicious ghosts or spirits, and on its far side they found themselves on the western fringes of Cathay. Marco described the religious practices of some of the Tibetan inhabitants of the region, who built many Buddhist monasteries and temples and used astrology to select the proper dates for their funerals. He mentioned as well the sexual practices common to some towns in the area, where guests were expected by custom to sleep with the married women; the excellent rhubarb grown in the mountains, which was still sought by Russian traders in the 19th century; and the manufacture of a substance he called "salamander," a cloth woven from threads of a fossil or mineral that could not be destroyed by fire. (He was describing asbestos, which was unknown in the West.)

After passing through this region, which Marco called Tangut, the Polos traveled north and east through Cathay proper toward Shang-du, Khubilai's summer capital. They arrived there in 1275, accompanied by the escort the Great Khan had sent to meet them. Their journey had taken three and a half years; Marco and his father and uncle had already seen more of Asia than any European before them. As they stood before Khubilai on that day, they had no idea just how much more of it they were destined to see or how long it would be before they saw their home again.

A 13th-century depiction of the arrival of the Polos at the court of Khubilai Khan. One of the older Polos is showing the khan the paizah the emperor had given them on their previous visit. The paizah was a flat plate of gold or silver with writing on it that ensured the bearer's safe conduct through the Mongol domains.

A Description
of the World

Although modern editions of Marco Polo's book have usually been entitled the *Travels*, the name that was given to the book when it was published during his lifetime was A *Description of the World*. The original title is better suited to the contents of the book because Marco's account of his experiences contains almost no personal narrative. Instead, the book consists of descriptions of as much of the world as Marco saw or heard about, sometimes in a rather haphazard order. It also contains a great deal of information about the history and customs of the Mongols, which Marco acquired from his hosts during his stay in the East, but the reader cannot always determine which of the places Marco talks about he actually visited or when he did so. Very little, in fact, is known about his life in China, and even less is known about how his father and his uncle spent their time there.

One thing that is known about Marco's experience at the Great Khan's court is that the young Venetian cleverly turned his talents for observation and description to his advantage. Not long after the Polos arrived in China, Khubilai sent Marco on an official mission of some sort, perhaps as an imperial representative or an emissary bearing official messages from the court. It is not clear whether this mission took Marco to Khorasan, in eastern Persia, or to a region that the Mongols called Kara-jang, which

Marco Polo in Tartar dress. It is not known to what extent, if any, Marco adopted Mongol customs while in China, but it is certain that he was a keen observer of life within the Mongol domains, and his curiosity and power of observation made him one of Khubilai's most trusted envoys.

A caravan wends its way along a precipitous pass in the mountains of Yunnan, a province in southwestern China to which Marco Polo may have traveled on his first diplomatic mission for the Great Khan. The name Yunnan means "beyond the clouds" in Chinese; at the time of Marco's visit China's rulers had been trying to conquer the remote region for almost 1,000 years.

is the present-day province of Yunnan in southeastern China, just north of Myanmar. Both regions are discussed at length in Marco's book, and it is clear that he visited or at least knew a great deal about both of them. At any rate, Marco traveled for six months to reach his destination, wherever it was, passing through regions that were inhabited by many different peoples. Upon returning to Khubilai's court at the conclusion of his mission, he was asked to make a report about his experiences. As the introductory section of his book explains:

> He had seen and heard more than once, when emissaries whom the Khan had dispatched to various parts of the world returned to him and rendered an account of the mission on which they had been sent but could give no other report of the countries they had visited, how their master would call them dolts and dunces, and declare that he would rather hear reports of these strange countries, and of their customs and usages, than the business on which he had sent them. When Marco went on his mission, being well aware of this, he paid close attention to all the novelties and curiosities that came his way, so that he might retell them to the Great Khan. On his return he presented himself before the Khan and first gave a full account of the business on which he had been sent—he had accomplished it very well. Then he went on to recount all the remarkable things he had seen on the way, so well and shrewdly that the Khan, and all those who heard him, were amazed and said to one another: "If this youth lives to manhood, he cannot fail to prove himself a man of sound judgment and true worth."

From that time on, Marco stood high in Khubilai's favor and was often sent on official business to various parts of the Mongol Empire and other countries. The Great Khan, pleased with Marco's entertaining and informative reports, "used to entrust him with all the most interesting and distant missions." It is for this reason, according to the introduction to his book, that Marco Polo "observed more of the peculiarities of this part of the world than any other man, because he traveled more widely in these outlandish regions than any man who was ever born, and also because he gave his mind more intently to observing them."

It is not known exactly what posts Marco held at court, but he does say that the Great Khan held him in high esteem and "kept him so near his own person that the other lords were moved to envy." Marco himself declared that he served as governor of the large and important city of Yangzhou for three years, between 1282 and 1285. This claim has been accepted at face value by most of Marco's biographers for centuries, but historian Morris Rossabi points out in *Khubilai Khan: His Life and Times* that the detailed Chinese administrative records of the period fail to show that Marco Polo ever served as governor of Yangzhou. It is possible that he held some other high post in the city, such as administrator of the very valuable salt trade, or that his name was somehow removed from the records.

Although doubt has been cast upon Marco's claim to have governed Yangzhou, it is clear that he was familiar with the city and at least visited it in the course of his duties. Yangzhou lies in the province of Jiangsu, in eastern China. In Marco's time, it was one of the major shipping ports on the Grand Canal, a marvel of engineering more than 1,000 miles long that connected the lower Changjiang River (sometimes referred to as the Yangtze) in south China with the Huanghe River (referred to in English for many years as the Yellow River) and the new capital of Khan-balik (modern-day Beijing) in the north. The Mongols did not build the Grand Canal—the oldest parts of it dated from the 5th century B.C.—but they improved and extended it. The channels cut under Khubilai Khan's supervision connected many existing rivers and lakes, said Marco, and the canal seemed like "a great river" on which large ships and barges could carry rice, charcoal, and other goods from one end of China to the other.

Marco Polo spoke often and with admiration of the ease of transportation, communication, and travel within the Mongol domain. He reported that the Mongols had repaired and extended the ancient Chinese road system, planting the highroads with shade trees along each side and paving them with brick and stone "so that it is possible to walk dry-shod throughout the length and breadth of the land"—something that could not be said of 13th-century Europe. It was also possible for messengers and travelers, including the imperial postmen, who jogged the three miles between post stations, to travel in safety, as the roads were regularly patrolled. Like Carpini and Rubruck before him, Marco noted that the post system allowed imperial messengers to travel with remarkable speed, and he added that fine palaces, complete with splendid beds and silk sheets, had been built for the use of the Great Khan's envoys at important stopping places and junctions along the roads. Furthermore, Khubilai had extended the post system into the mountainous and desolate regions on the edges of his empire. "The Great Khan sends people to live there and till the soil, performing the necessary services for the posts," Marco noted. "Thus large villages are formed."

During his years in China, Marco Polo visited many cities and provinces. He appears to have traveled fairly extensively in west-central China, in the regions that today are the provinces of Shaanxi, Shanxi, and Sichuan, and also to have visited the mountain kingdom of Tibet, which was for many centuries thereafter, largely because of Polo's descriptive powers, the typical Westerner's idea of the most remote place on earth. He described in great detail its "castles and strong towns, built upon rocky heights, or upon the summits of mountains." (Some of these were probably Buddhist monasteries, which were extremely numerous in Tibet.) He told how the Tibetans used bamboo, which grew in the eastern part of their country, to frighten away tigers and other wild beasts: They placed lengths of

bamboo cane in their fires at night, and the loud noise
that resulted when the heat of the flames caused the joints
of the cane to explode kept the predators at bay. He described a breed of large, hump-backed, shaggy-haired cattle that the inhabitants of the region used as beasts of
burden; these were the yaks that live in the Himalayas.
The Tibetans placed a high value on coral, he said, and
used it plentifully as decoration for their religious idols
and as women's jewelry—an observation echoed by many
later travelers. He also mentioned their clothing, made of
skins and furs, their interest in magic and sorcery, and
their large and fierce dogs (a breed of mastiff that still exists
in Tibet).

At the time of Marco Polo's arrival in China, the Mongols' power was greatest in the north, near their homeland;
the conquest of southern China was not completed until
1279. Marco apparently traveled widely in the north and
may even have visited Karakorum, the ancient Mongol
capital. He mentioned the Altai Mountains, and he reported that a journey of 40 days north from Karakorum

*While in the Great Khan's service
Marco visited the mountain
kingdom of Tibet, then as now
the most devoutly Buddhist
nation on earth. Marco described
the thousands of lamaseries, such
as the one pictured, that dot the
rugged Tibetan landscape. The
lamaseries are home to Tibet's
many lamas, as its Buddhist
monks are known.*

Marco was so enamored of the Chinese port city of Kinsai (modern-day Hangzhou) that he called it the City of Heaven. It no doubt reminded him of his home city of Venice, for Kinsai, like the Italian city-state, was a city of waterways traversed by bridges. "Of the noble and magnificent city of Kinsai . . . it is commonly said that the number of bridges, of all sizes, amounts to twelve thousand, for the most part so lofty that a great fleet could pass beneath them," Polo's narrative recounts.

brought the traveler to a region of "numerous lakes and marshes" filled with birds and inhabited by "a rude tribe" of people who lived by herding large animals that resembled stags. This was the first description of Siberia and its reindeer-herding peoples to reach the West. In another part of his book, Marco describes the dogsleds used to travel over snow and ice by some of the pale-skinned peoples of northern Russia. He also spoke of a northern "Land of Darkness"—the polar regions where winter night lasts for several months—and of a "northern ocean" that was "so far to the north that the polar star appears to be behind you"—the Arctic Ocean.

As far as Chinese cities were concerned, Marco Polo claimed that the coastal port of Hangzhou, which he called Kinsai, was "without doubt the finest and most splendid city in the world." His description of the City of Heaven, as he called Kinsai, was lengthy. The merchant in Marco dwelled lovingly upon the city's 10 spacious and busy marketplaces, its strong stone warehouses for goods, its bustling river docks, and the many items its traders offered for sale, ranging from huge, sweet pears to pearls and spices. The craftsmen and merchants of Kinsai, he reported, were organized into trade guilds, and the leading merchants and their wives "never soil their hands with work at all, but live a life of as much refinement as if they were kings." Marco also enjoyed the city's wholesome air, clean streets, and public baths, and he remarked with gusto that a fine meal could be made from its spiced wine and fresh fish. He described a beautiful, clear man-made lake on the southern side of Kinsai, around which stood "stately palaces and mansions." Many of these dwellings, as well as lavishly ornamented pleasure boats, could be hired for banquets and wedding feasts. "On the lake itself," he recalled, "is the endless procession of barges thronged with pleasure-seekers. For the people of this city think of nothing else, once they have done the work of their craft or their trade, but to spend a part of the day with their womenfolk or with hired women in enjoying themselves either in these barges or in riding about the city in carriages."

Outside China, Marco Polo's travels appear to have taken him to northern Burma, which he called Mien; to Cambodia or southern Vietnam, which he called Champa; and at least once to India. He devoted a large section of his book to India, drawing upon his own experience and the tales of other travelers. He described both the east and west—or Coromandel and Malabar—coasts and mentions more than once the fine cottons woven in many Indian cities. Showing an obvious familiarity with the customs of India, Marco told how followers of the Hindu religion ("idolaters" to him) showed reverence for oxen and refused to slaughter them and how the wives and servants of important men sacrificed themselves on their masters' funeral pyres. He described aspects of everyday life among the Indian people, who slept on light, portable beds of woven cane or rope and who liked to chew the leaf of the betel nut mixed with lime, a practice that is still popular throughout much of southern Asia. Marco paid great attention to the pearl fisheries of southern India, and he marveled at the skill and endurance of the divers who brought up the oysters that contained the precious gems. Of the island of Ceylon, he reported that it produced "more beautiful and valuable rubies than are found in any other part of the world, and likewise sapphires, topazes, amethysts, garnets, and many other precious and costly stones." This continual emphasis on the wealth of the East is part of what made Marco's narrative so appealing to generations of European readers.

Nicolo and Maffeo Polo also had good reason to admire the riches of the Orient. Marco's father and uncle may themselves have occupied some official positions in Khubilai's government. They may also have traveled around China; on at least one occasion, Marco refers to a trip he took with his uncle. Marco also claimed that Nicolo and Maffeo served as military advisers to Khubilai, helping him construct giant catapults to hurl boulders against the walls of the rebellious city of Xiangyang in southern China; this claim is dubious, however, because the siege of Xiangyang is known to have ended in 1273, two years before the Polos arrived in China. It is possible that Marco confused one military episode with another in which his father and uncle did take part. At any rate, Nicolo and Maffeo Polo carried on a number of profitable trading ventures during their time in China, probably with the approval or even the help of the Great Khan, and they accumulated a notable store of wealth "in jewels of value and in gold," as Marco described it.

The Mongol Empire reached its greatest extent under Khubilai's rule. At its height, it included all of present-day China, Mongolia, Korea, Afghanistan, Iran, and Iraq and parts of Siberia, Russia, Turkey, Syria, Pakistan, and India. Myanmar, Vietnam, and Cambodia were not officially part of the empire, but their sovereigns paid tribute to the Great Khan and admitted his superiority, as did

This pastoral scene from an 8th-century Indian miniature probably depicts a religious celebration. If the material devoted to it in A Description of the World *is any indication, Polo apparently traveled extensively in India. He commented on the Indian devotion to cattle; Hindus associate bulls with Siva, the god of destruction, and cows with the earth and thus forbid the eating of beef.*

many Indian princes. Of nearby lands, only Japan proved able to resist Khubilai's might. The Great Khan tried several times to conquer this stubbornly independent island kingdom, which Marco called Zipangu, losing in the process two battle fleets to storms and Japanese warriors. Marco, however, was able to draw upon the recollections of Mongol soldiers and envoys to paint a fairly detailed picture of Japan, which was utterly unknown in the West before his book was published.

Much of Marco Polo's book is not concerned with geography or warfare or business, however, but with the Mongols themselves and their Chinese subjects. Pages are devoted to descriptions of Khubilai's palaces, the etiquette and operation of his court, his sophisticated system of government, Mongol history and customs, and the genealogy of the imperial Mongol family. Some of Marco's descriptions of what the Chinese themselves would have regarded as the more mundane aspects of their lives, such as the use of gunpowder, the burning of coal for fuel, and their fondness for noodles, would prove to be among the most influential passages of his work, as neither coal, gunpowder, nor noodles (from which the Italians developed pasta) were widely known in the West. Marco's description of Khubilai's government monopoly on the use of gold and silver and the resulting widespread use of paper currency would also greatly influence the course of Western cultural development. Although most of Marco's detailed observations have been confirmed by later travelers and historians, there are some significant errors and omissions in his account. For example, he identifies Ong Khan, a contemporary of Chinggis's, as the mythical Christian monarch Prester John, and he fails to mention at all Ögödei Khan, Chinggis's successor. Despite these and other flaws, however, his account of Khubilai Khan and the Mongols at the height of their power is an unparalleled look at a remarkable leader and his extraordinary government of the largest land empire in world history.

Marco Millions

The Polos prospered during their stay in China, and Marco, at least, seems to have enjoyed it, but as time went on the Venetians yearned for home. Furthermore, Khubilai—who was born in 1215—was getting on in years, and by the mid-1280s he was no longer in the best of health. The favoritism that the khan had shown toward the Polos had earned them enemies among the powerful nobles of his court, and the Italians feared that if he died before they left China, they might have trouble getting themselves and their valuables safely out of the country.

With this thought in mind, Nicolo Polo waited for a day when Khubilai was "more than usually cheerful," according to Marco, and asked the Great Khan for permission to return home. Khubilai "appeared hurt at the application, and asked what motive they could have for wishing to expose themselves to all the inconveniences and hazards of a journey in which they might probably lose their lives." The khan offered to give them double the value of all their possessions if they wished to increase their wealth, but he refused them permission to depart.

The Polos then received help from an unexpected source. In 1286, the wife of Arghun, the khan of Persia, died. On her deathbed, she begged her husband to take as his next wife only a member of her own family—that is, the Mongol royal family descended from Chinggis Khan. Arghun sent envoys to Khan-balik to ask Khubilai to send him a Mongol princess to wed, and the Great Khan selected a young woman of his family named Kokachin. The princess, Arghun's envoys, and their escort

A soulful Marco Polo as he might have looked in later years while remembering his days in the realm of the Great Khan. Many of his fellow citizens regarded Marco's tales of his adventures as the fabrications of a liar or the ravings of a madman, but he insisted that he had not told the half of what he had seen.

set off overland for Persia, but after eight months of travel they found their way blocked by regional warfare that had broken out among the princes of the western khanates. They returned to Khan-balik and announced that they would prefer to travel to Persia by sea, around the Malay Peninsula and India. At about this same time, Marco returned to the Great Khan's court from a sea voyage, perhaps to India or the coast of Southeast Asia. Arghun's messengers had heard that Marco was a seasoned traveler, and they begged the Great Khan to let him escort them to Persia. Khubilai reluctantly agreed. It thus happened that Marco Polo, who had reached the East along one of the two great trade arteries of the ancient world, the Silk Road, returned to the West along the other, the Spice Route.

Khubilai furnished the three Polos with the paizah that ensured their safe conduct throughout his realm, and he made them promise to visit him again once they had delivered the princess to Arghun and visited their home in

While a crowd of curious onlookers watches, Marco and Maffeo Polo are turned away from the family home upon their return to Venice. If legend is to be believed, it was only when the Polos slit open their Tartar robes to reveal a prince's ransom in diamonds and gems that the long-lost strangers were recognized and allowed entrance. This woodcut is from a 19th-century English version of Marco's book.

Venice. Then he put at their disposal a fleet of 14 ships, several of which were large enough to require a crew of 250 men. The fleet embarked in 1291 or 1292 from Amoy, a port in the present-day province of Fujian in southern China. (This voyage and Marco's earlier sea journeys gave him the opportunity to report on Chinese shipbuilding and seamanship, of which he formed a high opinion.) After sailing southwest through the South China Sea, the fleet reached Java three months after leaving Amoy. In his book, Marco Polo described the kingdoms and products of this Indonesian island and also those of Sumatra, Malaya, Ceylon, and India—all places where the fleet landed on its way to Persia. He spoke of the pirates that infested the eastern seas and preyed upon both Muslim and Chinese vessels; each year, he said, more than 100 pirate ships put out from the Gujarat kingdom of India alone. On the west coast of India, the fleet called at trading ports frequented by Arab seamen, and there Marco gathered information about places in the Indian Ocean and in Africa that he did not visit but described in his book. Among these places—some of which were first brought to the attention of Europeans by Marco—were the islands of Socotra, Zanzibar, and Madagascar and the African countries of Abyssinia (Ethiopia), Somalia, and Mozambique.

Approximately 30 months after leaving Amoy, the fleet arrived at Hormuz, on the Persian Gulf. Hundreds of Khubilai's sailors and soldiers had died on the way, but the three Polos and Kokachin, their charge, had survived, only to learn that Arghun Khan had died and that Kokachin was now to be married to his son Ghazan. After the Polos delivered the princess to her bridegroom—Marco said that she had become so fond of her Venetian guardians that she wept upon parting from them—they spent nine months resting from the journey in Tabriz, in northwestern Persia, where they received word that Khubilai had died in early 1294. This news, Marco wrote, "entirely put an end to all prospect of their revisiting those regions."

Benevolent winds blow Venetian vessels back to their home city, which is built on 118 tiny islands in a lagoon. Venice was forced to fight many wars to maintain its dominant position in the trade between Europe and Asia; in a battle with Genoa, its main rival, Marco Polo was taken captive.

The peripatetic Polos instead went north to the port of Trebizond, in eastern Turkey on the Black Sea, where they took ship for Constantinople. In this seven-hilled city, the so-called second city of Christendom, it was an easy matter for the Polos to get sea passage to Venice, where they arrived in 1295.

There is no surviving firsthand account of the Polos' return home after an absence of 24 years. John Baptist Ramusio, who wrote a biography of Marco Polo two centuries later, recounts a persistent legend that the three men, much aged, worn by their years on the road, and dressed in ragged, travel-stained garments, were rudely turned away from the gate of the Polo mansion. Family members, it is said, failed to recognize their long-lost kin and scornfully dismissed them as beggars, whereupon Nicolo, Maffeo, and Marco ripped open the seams of their filthy clothes and out poured streams of rubies, diamonds, and emeralds. At this, the harsh words with which the travelers had been greeted suddenly turned to warm welcomes, and the three were embraced and treated to a lavish and lively banquet.

Like all returned travelers, Marco Polo entertained his friends and family with tales of his adventures, but the rest of the world might never have heard his story had it not been for a war between the city-states of Venice and Genoa over control of the Mediterranean. During the conflict, Marco Polo served as a *sopracomito*, or "gentleman commander," aboard a Venetian galley. In September 1296, the Venetian and Genoese fleets engaged in battle off Curzola Island, near the coast of present-day Yugoslavia. The Venetians were defeated, and Marco Polo was among those taken to Genoa as prisoners.

Polo's captivity lasted less than a year, yet these months of imprisonment gave birth to one of the world's masterpieces. While a captive, Polo made the acquaintance of another prisoner, named Rustichello (or Rusticiano) of Pisa, who had achieved some notice as the author of romances in French about King Arthur and the Round Table. In the course of their conversations, Polo no doubt regaled his new friend with stories of his adventures in the East. Rustichello convinced the talkative Polo that his reminiscences would make a good book, and Polo sent to Venice for the notes he had made about his travels. With Marco Polo providing the substance and Rustichello the literary touch (and some license), A *Description of the World* was written. Within a century or so it had been translated into most European languages. Since the 16th century, it has never gone out of print.

Scholars have never been able to determine exactly what Marco Polo told Rustichello or what Rustichello added to the story on his own account. At least 85 early manuscripts exist, and each differs from the others to some degree.

Some contain long passages not found in other versions, and it appears that certain translators and editors may have added material from other sources. Rustichello himself is believed to have added (or at least embroidered) some of the chapters that have a fairy-tale quality, including the accounts of religious miracles similar to those found in many legends of Persia and the Levant. The descriptions of Mongol battles that fill the final chapters of the book are also thought to be largely the creation of Rustichello's imagination, as they bear a suspicious resemblance to chapters from some of his own earlier romances. All that can be said with certainty is that the book was a true creative collaboration in which the separate contributions of the two authors cannot always be identified.

Debate has always raged over Marco Polo's truthfulness. In his own time, most people thought that he was a spinner of yarns who exaggerated his travels and the things he had seen for the sake of a good story. He was nicknamed *Il Milione*, which is usually translated as Marco Millions, partly because he was thought to be a millionaire and partly because people teased him about having a million made-up stories to tell. Later, skeptical travelers and scholars wondered why, if he had spent so many years in China, his account makes no mention of such obvious facts of Chinese life as tea, the binding of the feet of upper-class

Marco's father and uncle receive the paizah from Khubilai Khan's aide in this illustration from a 14th-century manuscript version of Marco's narrative. Within several decades of its appearance, Marco's book had been translated into virtually all of the major European languages, including Gaelic.

women, and the Great Wall of China. Polo's supporters, on the other hand, argue that it is quite possible that portions of the original manuscript have been lost. Furthermore, they point out, Polo *does* describe a number of things that were unique to China at the time, such as the burning of coal for fuel and the printing and use of paper money. The historian Herbert Franke has summed up the most common scholarly opinion regarding Marco Polo's reliability this way: "Until definite proof has been adduced that the Polo book is a world description, where the chapters on China are taken from some other, perhaps Persian, source (some of the expressions he uses are Persian), we must give him the benefit of the doubt and assume that he was there after all."

The later life of Marco Polo, like his childhood, is shrouded in obscurity. It is known that he carried on a moderately profitable trading business, dealing principally in Russian furs and English tin, and that he married a Venetian noblewoman named Donata Badoer, with whom he had three daughters. The girls, who were named Fantina, Bellela, and Moreta, had six children, four girls and two boys. All of them are mentioned in Polo's will, which states that his estate is to be divided among his three daughters. The will also instructs that Polo's Tartar slave, Peter, is to be set free upon his master's death, but no other mention of Peter exists, and his history and fate are unknown.

Marco Polo died on January 9, 1324, and was buried in the Church of San Lorenzo in Venice. A story first told by a 14th-century writer named Jacopo d'Acqui holds that when Marco, on his deathbed, was urged by his children to confess to having made up his remarkable tales, he replied that he had not told half of what he had seen and done. No portrait was made of him during his lifetime, although he was portrayed by many later artists; a painting of him dating from the 16th century, 200 years after his death, is the oldest known to survive.

Whether read for entertainment or for information, Marco Polo's book has enthralled readers for 700 years. Yet his achievement is not solely a literary one, for he is one of a handful of individuals who reshaped the way humanity thinks of the world and its peoples. At a time when the people of Europe were largely fearful of other races and cultures, he showed that Westerners and Easterners could understand and even grow to like one another. Indeed, his book suggested that people everywhere, whatever the apparent differences in their customs and appearances, are subject to the same needs and emotions. He made the farthest reaches of Asia accessible to the inhabitants of the small, familiar world of Europe, and the amount of clear, accurate information he conveyed far outweighs the occasional errors and fabrications. Not long after his death, two important sets of maps—the *Laurentian* (or *Medicean*) *Atlas*, completed in 1351, and the *Catalan Atlas*, completed in 1375—reflected the changes he had wrought in the Western view of the world. In their attempts to reproduce real, practical geography instead of biblical dogma or legend, both show Marco Polo's influence. The *Catalan Atlas*, in particular, shows central Asia and China very much as they are described by Polo. Almost until the modern era—certainly through the Renaissance—Marco Polo's descriptions remained Europe's primary source of information about Asia.

Perhaps the most important effect of Polo's book was the inspiration it provided to other travelers. His descriptions of the bazaars of the East, overflowing with gems and silks, and of the rich islands of Zipangu and Ceylon fired the greed of merchants and the imaginations of explorers. No less important an explorer than Christopher Columbus owned a copy of A *Description of the World*. Its margins were filled with notes written in Columbus's own hand, and Polo's estimate of the extent of Asia's landmass, which far exceeded the calculations of previous geographers, was crucial in convincing Columbus that it was possible to reach the East by sailing west. Thus, Polo's description of a world then almost entirely new to Europeans can be said to have been instrumental in enabling Europeans to discover the New World. This is a legacy of which Marco Polo himself, with his relentless curiosity and appetite for adventure—two primary attributes of any great explorer—would no doubt have been proud.

The publication of A Description of the World *added immeasurably to the store of geographic knowledge available to Europeans. The* Catalan Atlas, *a* mappamundi *(map of the world) made for the king of Aragon by the Jewish cartographer Abraham Cresques in 1375, reflected Marco's revelations about the Asian continent. This detail from the atlas shows the Great Khan at lower right, in tent; the city of Kinsai can be seen at center, below the white elephant.*

The Last Medieval Travelers

Although Marco Polo is certainly the best-known traveler of his time, many other European explorers followed in his footsteps, so to speak, and made their way to Asia. Some of them were missionaries, continuing the effort to Christianize the East that began with Carpini and Rubruck. Even before the return of the Polos, in 1289 Pope Nicholas IV sent an Italian Franciscan friar named John of Montecorvino to China. Six years later, he arrived in Khan-balik, where he claimed to have baptized 6,000 Chinese and Mongols and to have founded a choir for the singing of Christian hymns. In recognition of his services to the church, the pope made Montecorvino the first Roman Catholic archbishop of Beijing in 1307.

Another Italian Franciscan, Odoric of Pordenone, lived in China for three years in the 1320s. After his return to Italy in 1330, Odoric dictated a detailed account of his time in the East. Yet another Italian friar, one John Marignolli, visited Beijing in 1342. He wrote of the several fine Christian churches that had been built there and reported that the small colony of European Christians living in China was held in high esteem by the Mongol khans.

Merchants as well as missionaries made their way eastward, many of them carrying a book written by an Italian merchant, Francesco Balducci Pegolotti, between 1334

The Italian friar Odoric of Pordenone kneels to receive his orders from Pope John XXII, who charged him with a diplomatic mission to China in the 1320s. According to Odoric, "Indeed in that country [China] the number of people is so great that among us here it would be deemed incredible; and in many parts I have seen the population more dense than the crowds you see at Venice on Ascension Day."

and 1342. Pegolotti worked for the Bardi, a powerful merchant clan of Florence. Based on his years of travel and trade on Bardi business, Pegolotti's volume was a handbook for traders, filled with practical advice: how to obtain a reliable guide across the steppes of Russia, for example, or how to bribe customs officials so that they will thereupon behave "with great civility" toward the traveling man of business. Pegolotti's handbook describes in detail the way stations and trading posts along the most northerly branch of the Silk Road across Eurasia, from Sarai on the Volga River through Turkestan to China, with tips on everything from transportation and food to clothing and entertainment. It contains as well a glossary of useful terms in several Asiatic languages and a table for converting various currencies, weights, and measures. The very existence of such a pragmatic guidebook suggests that just a few decades after Marco Polo's epic journey, transcontinental travel had become somewhat less than extraordinary, if not yet merely commonplace.

Yet even while Europeans were assimilating the idea of Asia into their worldview, tremendous changes were taking place on the far side of that continent. The mighty Mongol Empire, which had been founded by Chinggis and expanded to its farthest reaches by Khubilai, began to fragment not long after Khubilai's death. The Mongol rulers had always been greatly resented by the native Chinese, who steadily grew increasingly rebellious, to the extent that by the middle of the 14th century the Mongols were beginning to lose control of China and the Pax Mongolica had almost reached its end. The era of great overland journeys made by Europeans to the East was virtually over; not until the end of the 15th century and the great exploratory sea voyages made by Portugal's master mariners would European merchant adventurers again visit the fabulous Asian realms in significant numbers. But in the meantime, two non-European travelers—Ibn Battuta, a North African legal official; and Cheng Ho, a Chinese admiral and eunuch—would complete a series of journeys that made them as adventurers every bit Marco Polo's equal, although their names are nowhere near as well known in the West as his.

Ibn Battuta was born in 1304 in Tangier, Morocco. His family had produced many *qadis* (Islamic judges), and he was accordingly well educated in Islamic literature and law. At age 21 he left home to make a *hajj*, the ritual pilgrimage to the holy city of Mecca, the home of the prophet Muhammad, that is one of the duties of every devout Muslim. On the way, he made a number of side trips: along the Nile River in Egypt; to the shores of the Red Sea; and, most important, to the city of Damascus, in Syria, where he studied with many noted Islamic scholars and religious mystics.

Learned Muslims of the Middle Ages drew upon a rich heritage of historical and geographic writings in Arabic, and it is likely that in Damascus or elsewhere Ibn Battuta encountered the work of earlier Muslim geographers such as al-Biruni, who, in the 11th century, several hundred years before Portuguese navigators "discovered" such a passage, speculated that a sea route existed around the southern tip of Africa; and al-Idrisi, a 12th-century Arab geographer who made a map of the world for the king of Sicily. Although he drew no maps of his own, as far as is known, Ibn Battuta was to become the best-traveled Muslim geographer of all time. The Islamic Marco Polo, as he is sometimes known, logged more miles than any known traveler of the Middle Ages. After completing his hajj, Ibn Battuta crossed Arabia and traveled in Persia and Russian Turkestan, near the Black and Caspian seas. Later he sailed south in the Red Sea and along the east coast of Africa as far as the Arab trading town of Kilwa, in present-day Tanzania, returning by way of Persia to Mecca in 1332. From there he decided to visit Delhi, in India, which was ruled by a Muslim sultan reputed to be very generous to visiting scholars. He took a somewhat wayward route to India, through Egypt, Syria, and Turkey into the khanate of the Golden Horde, from where he made a side trip to Constantinople as a companion to the khan's wife, after which he finally proceeded east and south across central Asia toward India at the head of a large caravan of his slaves, followers, wives, and concubines. While passing through Bukhara, Samarkand, and Balkh, he noted the devastation left by the conquering Mongol hordes several generations earlier. Bukhara, he wrote, had been "laid in ruins by the accursed Tankiz [Chinggis]"; Samarkand, once "one of the greatest and finest cities, and most perfect of them in beauty," in which "there were formerly great palaces on its bank, and constructions which bear witness to the lofty aspirations of the townsfolk," had been mostly obliterated, and much of the city had fallen into ruins.

Sometime in the mid-1330s, Ibn Battuta finally arrived in Delhi, where he managed to secure the post of qadi for the city. His account of his years in service to the sultan of Delhi form the most interesting portion of his memoirs, for Muhammad ibn Tughluq was a despotic ruler, cruel

A map of Egypt, showing it divided by the Nile River and surrounded by the Mediterranean, by the 12th-century Arab geographer al-Idrisi. While Europe was suffering its Great Interruption of geographic knowledge during the Middle Ages, learned Arabs were avidly pursuing the earth's secrets.

and capricious, who both fascinated and terrified Ibn Battuta, who recalled later that "there was no day that the gate of his palace failed to witness alike the elevation of some object to affluence and the torture and murder of some living soul." Although many of the traveler's friends and fellow scholars fell afoul of the sultan and were executed, Ibn Battuta somehow managed to remain in his good graces, but when, in the early 1340s, he was named Delhi's envoy to China, he fled the sultan's court as swiftly as politesse would allow. On the way to China he suffered a series of misadventures involving pirates, local wars, shipwrecks, a marriage, and sojourns in the Maldive Islands and on Sumatra. He claims to have at last landed at Amoy, the port from which the Polos embarked on their return journey, and to have traveled by canal and river as far north as Beijing, but this portion of Ibn Battuta's story is brief and plagued with inconsistencies, and scholars are still debating the accuracy of his statements.

Upon leaving China, Ibn Battuta sailed by way of the Spice Route to Baghdad and then went north into Syria, where in 1348 he witnessed the ravages of the bubonic plague, called the Black Death, which was soon to sweep across Europe. He revisited Egypt, made yet another pilgrimage to Mecca, and finally returned to his homeland in North Africa around 1349, after an absence of 25 years. He was not done wandering, however; he had vowed to visit all the principal Muslim countries of the world, and there were a few yet to see. In 1350, he crossed the Mediterranean Sea to visit the kingdom of Granada, in Spain, the last stronghold of the once extensive Moorish Empire on the Iberian Peninsula. Several years later he made his last journey, which led him south across the Sahara Desert to the African kingdom of Mali, a nation of Muslims of mixed black and North African descent. Mali's capital was the legendary city of Timbuktu, which had long been a trading center for the camel caravans that snaked across the empty Sahara Desert laden with gold, salt, ivory, and

A Chinese junk of the 13th century. Marco Polo was astonished by the tremendous size of Chinese ships, which he described as typically containing 50 or 60 small cabins inhabited by a trader and his goods. The ships of Cheng Ho's fleet were described as being of 1,000 tons or more; at the time, the largest European vessel was about 100 tons.

slaves. The guide who led Ibn Battuta's caravan across the scorching sands was blind; he set his course by smelling the sand at the end of each day's travel.

Ibn Battuta returned from Mali to Morocco in late 1353. At the request of his country's sultan, he dictated an account of his life's journeys, during the course of which the Traveler of Islam is thought to have covered more than 75,000 miles and to have met at least 60 kings, khans, or sultans. He died in 1369 and was buried in Tangier, his birthplace. His book, called the *Rihlah* (Travels), was regarded by his contemporaries as a fictional romance and was almost forgotten until French scholars working in Algeria rediscovered it in the 19th century. Today, with most of its contents supported by other historical records, the *Rihlah* is regarded as a unique account of life in many parts of the far-flung world of medieval Islam. It is particularly valuable to scholars who are still piecing together the histories of the powerful and sophisticated African cultures, such as the kingdom of Mali, that are now known to have existed south of the Sahara in medieval times.

Although he made many sea voyages, Ibn Battuta is remembered primarily as an overland traveler. Several decades after his death, another Muslim adventurer, Cheng Ho, established himself as the foremost seafarer of medieval times. Cheng Ho was named Ma Ho at his birth in 1371 in Yunnan, a southern province of China that had not yet been subdued by the Chinese successors to the deposed Mongol rulers of the country. His family was prominent in the local Muslim Mongol community: His father had made the hajj to Mecca, and the family claimed to be descended from a former Mongol governor of Yunnan and from a king named Muhammad who had once ruled Bukhara—the family name Ma was said to be a shortened form of "Muhammad." In 1381, when forces loyal to China's new ruling family, which would go down in history as the Ming dynasty, conquered Yunnan, the 10-year-old Ma Ho was captured, castrated, and forced into the Ming army. He proved an adept soldier and by 1390 had become a junior officer with important friends at the Ming court. (Traditionally, many positions of power and influence in the Chinese court were held by eunuchs—castrated men.)

In 1402, a Ming prince named Chu Ti, who was a friend of Ma Ho's, named himself Emperor Yung-Lo. The new emperor was determined to establish the Ming as China's rulers in the eyes of the world. Years of fighting in China and elsewhere in the Mongol Empire had loosened the ties of respect and tribute that had bound much of Asia to China during Khubilai's lifetime, and Yung-Lo wanted to restore China's prestige. He decided that a series of ambitious naval expeditions would impress the world with China's might and wealth, and he selected Ma Ho to be commander in chief of these missions to what the Chinese called "the western oceans," favoring him with the new surname Cheng.

The first of Cheng Ho's naval expeditions set sail in 1405. It consisted of 62 ships carrying 27,800 men. (One of his later expeditions consisted of 317 ships and 37,000 men.) Earlier travelers, including Marco Polo and Ibn Battuta, had remarked upon the great size of Chinese sailing ships, but those built for Cheng Ho's fleet were among the largest of all time. The biggest were called treasure ships; they had 9 masts and were 444 feet long. The intermediate rank of vessels were called horse ships, supply ships, and billet ships. The smallest were the combat ships, which had 5 masts and were 180 feet long. All of Cheng Ho's vessels were considerably larger than any existing European ships.

On the first expedition, the fleet called at ports in Champa (southern Vietnam), Thailand, Malaya, Java, India, and Ceylon before returning to China in 1407. The expedition's purpose was neither conquest nor trade but to demonstrate, through its sheer magnitude, Chinese superiority, to overawe the inhabitants of the lands it visited with incontrovertible proof of China's power and might. Cheng Ho gave costly and elaborate gifts to the rulers of the countries he visited, and he offered to take envoys back to China, but he made no direct attempts to intimidate his hosts. Nor did he have to. The threat was implicit in the presence of such an awesome fleet.

Cheng Ho's second voyage, which took place in 1409, proved less peaceful. The Chinese admiral was forced to battle King Alagonakkara of Ceylon, who apparently had attempted some kind of treachery or betrayal, and took the king captive back to China. The third voyage began in 1411 and took Cheng Ho to Hormuz and the Persian Gulf; on his return journey, he landed at Sumatra. The fourth voyage began in 1413. Once again Cheng Ho touched at a number of Asian ports and then went on to Hormuz, but this time he continued south along the coast of Arabia to Aden, while a delegation from the fleet visited Mecca and Egypt by land. The fleet then cruised the east African coast, stopping at Malindi and other ports and reaching almost as far south as the Mozambique Channel between

Madagascar and the African mainland. Cheng Ho returned to China in 1415, accompanied by envoys from more than 30 nations that wished to pay homage to Emperor Yung-Lo.

The Three-Jewel Eunuch, as Cheng Ho was known to his contemporaries, made his fifth voyage—once again to the Persian Gulf and the east coast of Africa—between the years 1417 and 1419. In 1421 he set sail for the sixth time in order to take all the foreign envoys home. This sixth voyage lasted for 2 years, during which the fleet touched at ports in 36 countries, from the island of Borneo in the east to Zanzibar in the west.

Emperor Yung-Lo died in 1424. With his patron gone, Cheng Ho found his influence at court diminished. He occupied a minor army position for several years until, in the winter of 1431, he was ordered by the new emperor, Hung-Hsi, to make a seventh expedition, for the purpose

The spirit of war, from a Ming dynasty scroll. Not long after Cheng Ho's voyages overawed China's neighbors, the Middle Kingdom, as China referred to itself, withdrew into an all but impenetrable isolation, but European monarchs, merchants, and adventurers never stopped trying to reach the East.

of establishing formal diplomatic relations with a number of states. Cheng Ho's final and farthest-ranging voyage took him to Borneo, Southeast Asia, India, Persia, Arabia, and Africa. He returned to China in 1433, where, shortly before his death two years later, he summed up his achievement in these words:

> The countries beyond the horizon and at the ends of the earth have all become subjects; and to the most western of the western or the most northern of the northern countries, however far they may be, the distances of the routes may be calculated. . . . We have traversed more than one hundred thousand *li* [a Chinese measurement equaling about a third of a mile] of immense water spaces and have beheld in the ocean huge waves like mountains rising sky-high, and we have set eyes on barbarian regions far away hidden in a blue transparency of light vapors, while our sails, loftily unfurled like clouds, day and night continued their course, rapid like that of a star, traversing the savage waves as if we were treading a public thoroughfare.

Although his enemies at court destroyed most of Cheng Ho's papers, plaques that he erected and temples built to commemorate his voyages still stand in India and Southeast Asia.

Cheng Ho's treasure fleets, as his flotillas were called, were the last effort that China made to maintain contact with the rest of the world. After 1433, the Ming dynasty withdrew into an impenetrable isolation. The Chinese people were forbidden to leave their country, and very few foreigners were allowed to enter. Those who were permitted to visit China were closely supervised by imperial monitors and restricted to certain port cities.

At about the same time, the rest of the former Mongol Empire, torn by warfare, was fragmenting into smaller states. The well-traveled roads that had carried Marco Polo and his like across western and central Asia became increasingly difficult to traverse, especially for Europeans, as many of the new Islamic states that arose in these regions were hostile to Christianity. Overland trade between Europe and Asia diminished. Once again, as during the Dark Ages, East and West were cut off from one another.

But whereas during the Dark Ages much of the geographic information that Europeans had obtained in previous centuries was lost and had to be rediscovered by a new generation of explorers, this was not the case after China retreated into its isolation in the mid-15th century. By that time, goods from the East, spices in particular,

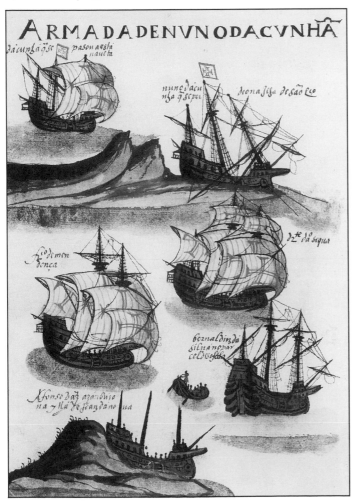

Portuguese caravels of the 15th century, the legendary sailing vessels with which that tiny seafaring nation ushered in a new era of exploration.

had become such an integral part of everyday European
life that continued contact with Asia, at least in the eyes
of traders and merchants, remained absolutely essential.
Some trade with the East, conducted through mostly Islamic middlemen in the Levant, continued, but the race
was on to discover a new route to the East—one that would
enable Europeans to reach China, India, and the nearby
regions directly. Traditionally, those Mediterranean cities
that controlled the spice trade with the Middle East, in
particular Venice and Genoa, had been Europe's most
prosperous and powerful, but a new age was dawning: The
future would belong not to those states that dominated the
Mediterranean but to those that looked outward, into the
Ocean Sea, as the Atlantic was then known. Foremost
among them was Portugal, continental Europe's westernmost nation. Portugal is tiny, but its coastline, for the most
part, faces west—outward, away from the Mediterranean
and toward the Atlantic. By the time China was closing
itself to outside contact and Constantinople was falling to
the Ottoman Turks, an Islamic power, in 1453, Portugal's
mariners were well on their way to "discovering" what was
for them a new route to the East—southward, by ship,
through the Atlantic Ocean and around Africa's southernmost tip, then eastward to the Malabar Coast, the Spice
Islands, and beyond. This same desire for an alternate sea
route to Asia would in 1492 lead Spain, Portugal's neigh-
bor and rival on the Iberian Peninsula, to sponsor a voyage
by an obscure Italian seaman, Christopher Columbus by
name, who claimed that he could reach China by sailing
due west across the Ocean Sea. The search for a new sea
route to the Indies, as Europeans referred to the islands
that they believed lay in the general vicinity of India,
ushered in a new era of exploration, one that culminated
in the discovery and exploration of lands as exotic, wealthy,
and beautiful as any visited by Marco Polo, truly unknown
to any but their inhabitants: the New World of the
Americas.

Further Reading

Battuta, Ibn. *Travels*, A.D. *1325–1354*. 3 vols. Translated by H. A. R. Gibb. Cambridge, England: University Press, 1958–71.

Boorstin, Daniel J. *The Discoverers*. New York: Random House, 1983.

Boulnois, L. *The Silk Road*. Translated by Dennis Chamberlin. London: Allen & Unwin, 1966.

Buehr, Walter. *The World of Marco Polo*. New York: Putnam, 1961.

Cameron, Nigel. *Barbarians and Mandarins: Thirteen Centuries of Western Travelers in China*. Chicago: University of Chicago Press, 1970.

Dramer, Kim. *Kublai Khan*. New York: Chelsea House, 1990.

Frank, Irene, and David M. Brownstone. *To the Ends of the Earth: The Great Travel and Trade Routes of Human History*. New York: Facts on File, 1984.

Hudson, G. F. *Europe and China: A Survey of Their Relations from the Earliest Times to 1800*. Boston: Beacon Press, 1961.

Humphrey, Judy. *Genghis Khan*. New York: Chelsea House, 1987.

Komroff, Manuel. *The Travels of Marco Polo*. New York: Liveright, 1982.

Lattimore, Owen, and Eleanor Lattimore. *Silks, Spices, and Empire: Asia Seen Through the Eyes of Its Discoverers*. New York: Delacorte Press, 1968.

Lomask, Milton. *Great Lives: Exploration*. New York: Scribners, 1988.

Mirsky, Jeannette, ed. *The Great Chinese Travelers*. New York: Pantheon Books, 1964.

Pennington, Piers. *The Great Explorers*. London: Bloomsbury Books, 1979.

Polo, Marco. *The Travels*. 1908. Reprint. Edited by W. Marsden. Annotated by John Masefield. New York: Dorset, 1987.

Rossabi, Morris. *Khubilai Khan: His Life and Times*. Berkeley: University of California Press, 1988.

Rutstein, Harry, and Joan Kroll. *In the Feet of Marco Polo: A Twentieth-Century Odyssey*. New York: Viking Press, 1980.

Severin, Timothy. *The Oriental Adventure: Explorers of the East*. Boston: Little, Brown, 1976.

———. *Tracking Marco Polo*. New York: Bedrick Books, 1984.

Stefoff, Rebecca. *Mongolia*. New York: Chelsea House, 1986.

Wilford, John Noble. *The Mapmakers*. New York: Knopf, 1981.

Chronology

Entries in roman type refer to events directly relating to Marco Polo and the medieval explorers; entries in italics refer to important historical and cultural events of the era.

100s	*Wary of the expensive and often perilous sea routes to the East, Mediterranean merchants develop a land route across the Eurasian plain to China: the Silk Road, as it comes to be known, becomes a driving force in East-West trade*
600s	*The rise of Islam in western Asia cuts off travel and trade between Christian Europe and the Far East; the Chinese Buddhist Hsüan-tsang travels extensively in India and Central Asia*
1095	*Pope Urban II calls for a crusade to retake the Holy Land from the Muslim infidel; the Crusades establish a European presence in the Near East and set the stage for expeditions into Asia*
1211–23	*Chinggis Khan conquers China, Persia, and Russia; the rise and expansion of the Mongol Empire opens eastward land routes to Europeans*
1245–47	Giovanni di Plano Carpini and Benedict the Pole, two Franciscan friars, travel to the Mongol capital of Karakorum
1251	Khubilai, the grandson of Chinggis Khan, becomes governor of China
1253–55	William of Rubruck, a Franciscan friar, crosses Russia to reach Mongolia and returns to Europe with information about these lands
ca. 1254	Marco Polo is born in Venice, Italy
1259	Khubilai becomes Great Khan of the Mongols
1269	Marco Polo's father, Nicolo, and his uncle, Maffeo, return from their 15-year journey to the East, where they met Khubilai Khan
1271	Nicolo and Maffeo Polo, accompanied by Marco, set out to return to Khubilai's court along the ancient Silk Road route

1275–92	Arrive at Khubilai's court; travel and work in the service of the Great Khan
1294	Khubilai Khan dies
1295	The Polos arrive in Venice after a 24-year absence; a Franciscan friar named John of Montecorvino reaches China
1296	Captured during a war between Venice and Genoa, Marco Polo is imprisoned with a writer named Rustichello of Pisa, who writes an account of his travels and tales of foreign places; their collaboration, entitled *A Description of the World,* is widely read throughout Europe
1304	Ibn Battuta, the traveler of Islam, is born in Tangier
1307	John of Montecorvino is named the first Christian archbishop of Beijing
1324	Marco Polo dies in Venice
1325	At age 21, Ibn Battuta begins a series of journeys that eventually cover about 75,000 miles
1368	*The Mongol rulers of China are overthrown by the native Chinese, who establish the Ming dynasty*
1369	Ibn Battuta dies in Morocco
1405–33	A series of naval expeditions led by Cheng Ho demonstrate the power and influence of China's Ming dynasty to peoples from Borneo to the east coast of Africa
ca. 1418	*Prince Henry the Navigator of Portugal begins dispatching mariners southward on the Atlantic in search of new trade routes, thereby ushering in a new era of exploration*

Index

Picture Credits

Alinari/Art Resource: pp. 20, 21; Art Resource: pp. 52, 72, 80, 86, 91; Bibliothèque Nationale, Paris: cover (map), pp. 18, 57, 58–59, 60, 61 (top), 62–63, 78, 88; The Bodleian Library/Weidenfeld & Nicholson, Ltd.: p. 64; Bridgeman/Art Resource: pp. 61 (bottom), 71; The British Library, M. S. Sloane, 5232: p. 67; General Research Division, The New York Public Library, Astor, Lenox and Tilden Foundations: pp. 29, 30, 68, 69, 70, 74, 77, 84, 98; Giraudon/Art Resource: cover (portrait), pp. 12, 15, 22, 32, 34, 36, 43, 44, 55, 82, 92, 96, 101; Metropolitan Museum of Art, Gift of the Dillon Fund, 1973 (1973.120.3): p. 25; Metropolitan Museum of Art, Gift of Mrs. Edward S. Harkness (47.81.1): p. 47; Metropolitan Museum of Art, Rogers Fund 1912, (12.37.133): p. 14; The New York Public Library Picture Collection: p. 16; The Pierpont Morgan Library, man. #525, folio #46: p. 107; SEF/Art Resource: pp. 27, 65; Weidenfeld & Nicholson, Ltd.: pp. 38, 52, 72, 80, 86, 98

Rebecca Stefoff is a Philadelphia-based freelance writer and editor who has published more than 40 nonfiction books for young adults, including *Mongolia* in the Chelsea House PLACES AND PEOPLES OF THE WORLD series. Stefoff received her M.A. and Ph.D. degrees in English from the University of Pennsylvania, where she taught for three years.

William H. Goetzmann holds the Jack S. Blanton, Sr., Chair in History at the University of Texas at Austin, where he has taught for many years. The author of numerous works on American history and exploration, he won the 1967 Pulitzer and Parkman prizes for his *Exploration and Empire: The Role of the Explorer and Scientist in the Winning of the American West, 1800–1900*. With his son William N. Goetzmann, he coauthored *The West of the Imagination*, which received the Carr P. Collins Award in 1986 from the Texas Institute of Letters. His documentary television series of the same name received a blue ribbon in the history category at the American Film and Video Festival held in New York City in 1987. A recent work, *New Lands, New Men: America and the Second Great Age of Discovery*, was published in 1986 to much critical acclaim.

Michael Collins served as command module pilot on the *Apollo 11* space mission, which landed his colleagues Neil Armstrong and Buzz Aldrin on the moon. A graduate of the United States Military Academy, Collins was named an astronaut in 1963. In 1966 he piloted the *Gemini 10* mission, during which he became the third American to walk in space. The author of several books on space exploration, Collins was director of the Smithsonian Institution's National Air and Space Museum from 1971 to 1978 and is a recipient of the Presidential Medal of Freedom.